Derek A. Thorpe

December 1975

KU-406-177

Derek A. Thorpe

December 1975

BIRDS OF THE TROPICS

THE WORLD OF NATURE

BIRDS OF THE TROPICS

JOHN A. BURTON
Previously Information Officer
at the British Museum (Natural History)

With a foreword by Professor Dillon Ripley
President of the International Council for Bird Preservation
Secretary of the Smithsonian Institution, Washington D.C.

ORBIS PUBLISHING · LONDON

Contents

© Istituto Geografico De Agostini, Novara 1973
English edition © Orbis Publishing Limited, London 1973
Printed in Italy by IGDA, Novara
ISBN 0 85613 147 4

Foreword

by Professor S. Dillon Ripley
President of the International Council for Bird Preservation
Secretary of the Smithsonian Institution, Washington D.C.

Throughout the world no single area is more rich in its variety of birds than the tropical zone. Whereas many of us grow up enjoying birds in the temperate climates of Western Europe or America where it is relatively easy to see the species with which we have fallen in love as children, the tropical zone is more difficult as a bird-watchers' haven. Only in the broad savannah areas of Africa or the open forests of eucalyptus of Australia is it possible to see birds with the facility that temperate bird-watchers enjoy. However, birds of the tropics are splendid in their diversity and variety and the momentary glimpses are often utterly captivating. The wonder of the tropics to the naturalist is the diversity of species which occurs there. Nowhere else in the world are so many species crowded into a similar area. The answer is that in the tropics many species occur with relatively small populations whereas in temperate or colder zones of the Arctic and Antarctic fewer species occur with vastly larger populations. Thus to know the birds of the tropics is an intricate life-long career pursued by few and indulged in by relatively infrequent hobbyists.

Today, as the interest in the tropics grows, more and more field-guides and similar illustrated books are attempting to delineate the birds of the tropical forests and areas rarely penetrated before except by the occasional scientific explorer or museum collector. Such a task is a monumental one and many volumes will be needed to cover the variety of birds to be seen in the great areas of South America, Asia, Africa and the Australasian Islands.

The present text ably supplements this fascinating phenomenon of species diversity in the tropics by giving the reader a once-over of the total distribution of birds. As can be seen from the text each special area such as Australasia or the Oriental region has its particular families or groups of birds found nowhere else. The variety of pigeons, parrots and kingfishers in Australasia, for example, far exceeds the variety of the same families in other areas of the world. And yet, as Alfred Russel Wallace pointed out more than a hundred years ago, other species or groups of birds such as the pheasants failed to cross 'Wallace's Line' and are distributed in magnificent array in the Oriental region. In each one of these regions the same thing is true. Certain families are found uniquely, or else in extraordinary diversity in one area compared to the others. Of course the Neotropics are celebrated for their wealth of humming-birds and tanagers, and similarly the Ethiopian region has a greater diversity of sunbirds and small finches than anywhere else.

One of the sadnesses of such a volume is the contemplation of the rapid changes which are overtaking the tropics. A mere generation ago it was possible to look at the tropics as a vast reservoir, a pool of forms of life which could easily sustain the rest of the world in its evolutionary complexity. That is not true any more today with the extraordinary opening up of tropical forests through agriculture and lumbering interests. I am sure that it will not be long before a number of the species of birds described here will follow those others listed towards the end of the book, especially from Oceania, in the mournful trail towards extinction. It is likely that some birds in the Brazilian forest may have become extinct before science even knew of their existence, a quixotic fate from the point of view of the student of evolution. It is likely that island species will continue to decline at a relatively drastic rate. The author has pointed out some of the causes of this present decline and noted that opening up island groups such as the Seychelles or the Galapagos for tourists may have harmful effects on the fauna in spite of the advertisements of the local governments encouraging tourists to come and see their rare and strange animals!

The International Council for Bird Preservation has concerned itself for over fifty years with attempting to forestall situations detrimental to threatened birds. It is now more than ever time to remind ourselves that conservation activities coupled with new environmental laws must make a strong appeal to all concerned citizens. Only in this way will there be any hope of salvaging a remnant of the once fantastic diversity of the tropics for our children and our children's children to enjoy.

Index of Birds

Page references to photographs are printed in **heavy** type.

The Tropical Habitat

The tropics are truly paradise for birds and bird-watcher alike. In these regions a greater number of species are likely to be encountered in a smaller area than anywhere else in the world. It would be impossible to mention all the species in a book of this length – indeed to mention all the families alone would make a boring catalogue with little space for more than the briefest detail. What I have attempted to do is select some of the families characteristic of the major tropical regions of the world, and illustrate and describe in detail a selection of the more interesting and unusual species. The families which are endemic – and confined – to the tropics, together with those families which have proliferated in those regions, are the main subject matter.

The chapters are based loosely on the divisions of the world used by zoogeographers – zoologists studying the distribution of animals. They are as follows: Neotropical region – South and Central America together with the Caribbean Islands; Ethiopian region – Africa south of the Sahara together with Madagascar and south-eastern Arabia; Oriental region – India and the Far East, south of a line running approximately through the Himalayas; Australasian region – Australia, New Guinea, New Zealand, and their associated islands. In addition to these regions, which all have a considerable part of their area within the tropics, there are the Palearctic region – North Africa, Europe and Asia, and the Nearctic region – North America. The various oceanic islands show affinities with adjacent land masses, but they also have certain unique characteristics and so are dealt with separately.

Of all the habitats throughout the world, tropical rain forest is the richest both in quantity and variety of life. The birds are also often remarkably colourful and many species have developed elaborate plumes and complicated courtship displays – only in a habitat with a superabundance of food can birds afford to devote so much time to such activities. Ever since Europeans first started visiting the tropics they have been amazed and dazzled by the beauty of the birds and it is to be hoped that this book will convey some idea of the splendour and variety of tropical birds.

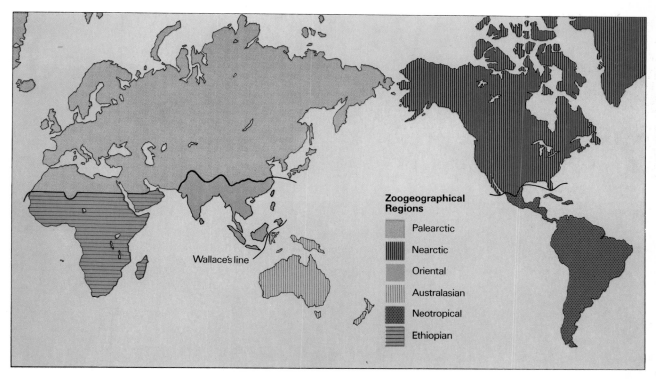

Wallace's line

Zoogeographical Regions

- Palearctic
- Nearctic
- Oriental
- Australasian
- Neotropical
- Ethiopian

THE AUSTRALASIAN REGION

From the tropical rain forests of New Guinea
to the deserts of Australia

The Australasian region comprises Australia, New Guinea, New Zealand and their associated islands as far north as the Celebes and Lombok – the region is separated from the Oriental region by 'Wallace's Line'. Either side of a gap between the islands of around 20 miles there is a remarkable difference between the two faunas, and the hypothetical line between them is named after Alfred Russel Wallace, the zoogeographer, who co-authored with Charles Darwin, the famous paper on the origins of species. This discontinuity in the faunas is explained by the fact that the islands to the north and west of Wallace's Line are part of the Asiatic continental shelf, and were connected with the Asiatic mainland during the periods of glaciation when sea levels dropped, whereas the islands to the south and east have long been isolated.

The Australasian fauna has many unique elements, including the birds of paradise and bower birds (Paradisidae), lyrebirds (Menuridae), megapodes (Megapodidae), magpie-larks (Grallinidae), honey-eaters (Meliphagidae), scrub-birds (Atricornithidae), cassowaries (Casuariidae), emu (Dromaiidae) and several others. The islands of New Zealand are considered to form a separate subregion within the Australasian region and they too have several characteristic families including the kiwis (Apterygidae), wattle-birds (Callaeidae) and New Zealand wrens (Xenicidae). In addition to families more or less confined to the region several others, although found in other parts of the world, show particular diversity in the Australasian region – the most notable being the kingfishers (Alcedinidae), pigeons and doves (Columbidae), and the parrots (Psittacidae).

One of the main reasons for the great differences of the Australasian fauna from that of the rest of the world is that it has been separated for a very long time, and that in isolation many groups have speciated. This is particularly so in the tropical forests of New Guinea.

Of all the tropical birds, the birds of paradise are undoubtedly the most spectacular, they convey to most people the image of an 'exotic' bird.

So impressed with them were the scientists and explorers who first named them in the 19th century that they often called them after the rulers and leading personages of their country – there are birds of paradise named by Germans after Princess Stephanie, Queen Carola, the King of Saxony, the Emperor of Germany, Count Raggi and others. The names of others contain superlatives – 'splendid' or 'magnificent' – suggesting how dazzled were their discoverers.

What are these 'birds of paradise' which cause such wonder? They are a family of birds confined to New Guinea and some adjacent islands – the early European traders in the East Indies were told that the birds had blown in from paradise. Only the males of the 40 or so species carry the elaborate plumes – the females tend to be rather similar to each other and dowdy. Although the males often look extremely different from each other they are in fact a fairly closely related group of birds; in the isolation of the mountain valleys of New Guinea they have evolved rapidly.

The beautiful plumes soon found a ready market in the western as well as the eastern world and a flourishing trade built up. By the beginning of the 20th century, tens of thousands of skins were being exported each year and some 30,000 were sold in London alone during 1913. But following a public outcry, in Britain and other countries, by 1924 the export of the plumes of birds of paradise had been completely outlawed.

The family to which the birds of paradise belong divides into two distinct groups – the birds of paradise, which have elaborate plumes in the males, and the bower birds, which lack the plumes but have interesting and complex nesting behaviour. Of the 42 species of bird of paradise, all but four are found in New Guinea, the others occurring in the Moluccas and Australia. The 18 species of bower bird are more widely distributed, 12 are from New Guinea, the rest from Australia.

Not all the birds of paradise have elaborate plumes – Loria's, the wattle-billed, Macgregor's and many others, lack the exaggerated plumes of some of the better known species. Those with

Primary rain forest in New Guinea. It is the luxuriant forests which provide the diverse habitats to support such a wide variety of bird species

3

well developed plumage do not necessarily develop the same feathers – in some it is the head or breast feathers while in others it is the tail or tail coverts. Wallace's standard wing (*Semioptera wallacei*) has two pairs of long white plumes coming out from the bend in the wing. The twelve-wired bird of paradise (*Seleucidis melanoleuca*) has tufts of black and yellow ornamental plumes on each side of the breast which include six wire-like projections on each side that sweep round in an arc to point forward. The black sickle-billed bird of paradise (*Epimachus fastosus*) – the largest species – has a long sweeping tail, and large fans of feathers (on either side of the breast) which can be erected during display.

The Arfak astrapia bird of paradise (*Astrapia nigra*) has a long, broad tail and extremely complex head plumage – like the other four species of

astrapia it has brilliantly iridescent plumage. The superb bird of paradise (*Lophorina superba*) has an enormous cape of feathers, springing from the back of the head, which covers almost the whole of the back. The six-wired birds of paradise (*Parotia* species) are characterized by having on each side of the head three wire-like projections with racquet-shaped ends – these wires are often nearly as long as the body. One of the most spectacular of all the species of birds of paradise is the King of Saxony bird of paradise (*Pteridophora alberti*). This species has a plume on either side of the head nearly twice the length of its body and tail. These two plumes are scalloped along their entire length and are a brilliant sky-blue in colour – they look as if they have been enamelled. The king bird of paradise (*Cicinnurus regius*) has the central pair of its tail feathers extended into wire-like projections,

which may be over five times the length of the rest of the tail, ending in emerald green circles of feathers. The magnificent bird of paradise (*Diphyllodes magnificus*) is one of the most colourful species, but it is probably the seven species of the genus *Paradisaea* which are the best known of all. In all these species the feathers on the sides of the flanks are developed into massive filmy tufts of feathers which are yellow, orange, red, white or blue, depending on the species. From the above descriptions it can be seen that the birds of paradise are truly remarkable in their plumage. What is the point of it all?

Very few of the birds of paradise have been observed in any great detail in the field but the few species for which observations have been made indicate that their behaviour is every bit as interesting as their plumage. Many of them are polygynous and the males live apart from the females, only contacting the females through an 'arena' display area. This type of behaviour is fairly rare in birds – in the grouse and ruff these displays are known as leks – and only two other groups of forest-dwelling birds are known to perform arena displays: the manakins and cotingas of the New World.

The nesting habits of the bower birds are as interesting as the plumages of their closer relatives. Although several of the bower birds are in fact quite brightly coloured, such as the golden regent bower bird (*Sericulus aureus*), it is their 'bowers' for which they are justly famous. These bowers are similar in function to the arenas of the birds of paradise, but the bower bird often actually builds and decorates an elaborate display area. The construction of the bower varies from species to species. For instance Archbold's bower bird (*Archboldia papuensis*) clears a ground court which it decorates with ferns, insects, snail shells, and yellowish vines; some of the gardener bower birds (*Amblyornis* species) build elaborate towers of sticks and twigs which may be up to five feet in diameter. The Australian regent bower bird (*Sericulus chrysocephalus*) not only builds a bower, but also paints it; it does this with a beak full of crushed vegetable matter.

Of the 300 species of pigeon some 44 occur in New Guinea, the most spectacular of which are the fruit doves. These are generally rather small – the dwarf fruit dove (*Ptilinopus nanus*) is only the size of a house sparrow, but like its other relatives it is extremely pretty. The males are a dark apple-green with grey and purple on the breast and yellow under the tail; when closed the wings appear blue-green tipped with yellow. Most of the other fruit doves found in New Guinea are similarly brightly coloured – the ornate fruit

(Right) male satin bower bird constructing his courtship bower in which he will display to attract a mate

(Left) little king bird of paradise

6

dove (*Ptilinopus ornatus*) for instance has the head a deep wine-red, followed by a blue-grey collar, grey throat and the top of the back and the sides of the neck dark brown to greenish-brown; the rest of the upper parts are green, with a dark red patch on the wings; there are orange and maroon bands on the breast, and the rest of the under parts are yellow. The fruit doves are found in Australia and many islands in South-East Asia and the Pacific as well as New Guinea.

Closely related to the fruit doves are the imperial pigeons. These birds are not quite so colourful as the fruit doves but they make up for this in size; the smallest is about the size of a racing pigeon – the largest, twice that of a wood pigeon.

Another group of large pigeons, confined to New Guinea and a few nearby islands, is the

(Left) green imperial pigeon, one of the larger of the groups referred to as fruit doves

(Left) crowned pigeon or goura of New Guinea —the largest member of the pigeon family, being around two and a half feet long

(Right) pair of Australian green-winged pigeons—one of the many species of pigeon found in the Australasian region. It is a member of the bronzewing group, rather partridge-like and largely ground-living

*Cockatoos are the
largest of the parrots
found in the Australasian
region, the largest
species being the great
black cockatoo*

spectacular goura, or crowned pigeon, (*Goura*
species). Among the largest members of the
pigeon family, the size of a chicken about two
feet long, they are basically a beautiful blue-grey
colour with elaborate lacy crests. The most
strikingly marked of the three species is the
maroon-breasted crowned pigeon (*G. cristata*)
which has a deep maroon breast. They are forest-
dwelling birds, with a deep, booming fog-horn-
like call, and are an impressive sight.

The parrots are among the most colourful
birds in the world and of the 316 species known,
some 46 are found in New Guinea. These range
in size from the tiny pygmy parrots (*Micropsitta*
species) smaller than a sparrow, to the massive
Palm cockatoos (*Probisciger aterrimus*), over two
feet long. Their diet ranges from nuts and berries
to bark, nectar, fungi and moulds, grubs and
carrion. The most colourful are probably the
lories (or lorikeets), such as the rainbow lory
(*Trichoglossus haematodus*). Several of the parrots
of New Guinea are also found in Australia, particularly Cape York; one of these, the eclectus
parrot (*Eclectus roratus*), shows extremely striking
plumage variation. The male is basically
green with a small amount of red and blue on the
wings; the female has a bright red head, maroon
wings, bright blue nape, belly and edge to wings.
This is one of the most extreme forms of sexual
dimorphism known in birds – usually the male is
the more brightly plumaged of the pair; in some
species such as the phalaropes the female is
brightly marked and the male dull, but in the
eclectus parrot, it is difficult to decide which of the
two is the more spectacular.

If the birds of paradise are the characteristic
birds of New Guinea, then parrots are the birds
which should be associated with Australia. In the

handbook to his *Birds of Australia* published in 1865, John Gould wrote: 'No group of birds gives so tropical and foreign an air as the numerous species of this great family . . . each and all of which are individually very abundant.' The 50 or so parrots found in Australia can be arranged in three groups: the lories (or lorikeets), the cockatoos, and the parrots (or parakeets).

The lories are brightly coloured – the most beautiful being the already mentioned rainbow lorikeet – and they have brush-like tongues which they use for feeding on nectar, blossoms, and soft fruits. They are often gregarious and the rainbow lorikeet can be found in gardens and parks. At Currumbin on the coast of southern Queensland, huge flocks of rainbow lorikeets, together with some scaly-breasted lorikeets come each day to a bird sanctuary to feed on honey solution put out by tourists.

The most impressive of Australia's parrot-like birds are undoubtedly the cockatoos. Probably the most beautiful is Leadbeater's cockatoo (*Cacatua leadbeateri*) known to Australians as Major Mitchell's cockatoo, after the famous explorer who was so impressed with the sight of these delicate pink birds which are found in the arid interior of Australia. The roseate, or galah as it is known in Australia, is almost as beautiful and is extremely common in certain areas. It is in fact the most abundant of the cockatoos, and since the beginning of this century has increased considerably. It is found mainly in savannahs and open grasslands and in many areas is shot by farmers as a pest. It has also colonized the area around towns and can even be seen in the centres of some towns, including Canberra.

Of the typical parrots, one species is known to everyone. This is the budgerigar (*Melopsittacus*

Lorikeets are a group of parrots in which the tongue is modified into a brush-like structure enabling them to extract nectar from blossoms. Violet-necked lorikeet is shown here

Purple-capped lorikeet

undulatus), found mainly in the arid interior of Australia, though rarely far from a supply of water where the birds will gather in flocks numbering many thousands in order to drink. Whilst some birds are settled around the edge of the waterhole drinking, others will alight on the surface of the water with their wings outstretched and drink while floating. Budgerigars have achieved their popularity partly on account of their ability (shared with many other parrots and cockatoos) to imitate human speech. The first person to discover this ability was probably a certain Thomas Watling who was deported to Australia in the famous 'Fleet of the Damned' for forgery. His abilities as a draughtsman led the surgeon of the penal colony to utilize his talents in recording the scenery and wildlife of the newly colonized territory, and Thomas Watling is believed to have kept a budgerigar which he taught to speak. John Gould, one of the most famous naturalists of the 19th century brought budgerigars back to Britain, and soon they were being imported in thousands. The budgerigar flourished, proving easy to breed in captivity, and there are now many pretty colour variants which bear little resemblance to their original wild ancestors.

The rosella parakeets (*Platycercus* species) rival the rainbow lorikeets for sheer brilliance of plumage. The exact relationship of all the species has yet to be fully understood as they intergrade and hybridize, causing many problems for the scientist. They show considerable variety in plumage colour – the green rosella (*P. caledonicus*) from Tasmania is pale green with blue and yellow markings, a red forehead and blue bib; the crimson rosella (*P. elegans*) from eastern Australia is bright red with blue bib, wings and tail; but the most beautiful of the group is the eastern rosella (*P. eximius*) which has a red head and breast, white bib and an orange underside which fades to yellow under the tail; the wings are blue with yellow and black markings and the tail green and blue.

The kingfishers (*Alcedinidae*) are found in many parts of the world, but of a world total of nearly 90 species over a third occur in the Australasian region – 24 species occurring in New Guinea alone. Many of the kingfishers are not the birds of rivers and streams so familiar to European birdwatchers, but rather omnivorous birds found in a wide variety of habitats. But like the European kingfisher many species are spectacularly plumaged; one of the most brilliant groups is the paradise kingfisher (*Tanysiptera* species). All but one of the eight species are confined to New Guinea; the eighth breeds in Australia and

13

winters in New Guinea. The paradise kingfishers can easily be distinguished from other kingfishers within their range by their long, central tail feathers, which in some species have enlarged tips. Their plumage colours include blues, blacks, pinks, browns, black and white, and both sexes are similar. Like most of the New Guinea kingfishers the paradise kingfishers are forest-dwellers and feed mainly on insects. The only species to breed in Australia (*Tanysiptera sylvia*) is restricted to the north-east where the suitable rainforest habitat occurs. Like so many of New Guinea's birds, little is known of their habits in that country, but in Australia they have been studied. It was found that although they spend most of their life near the top of the forest canopy, they nest close to the ground, often excavating their nest burrows in a termite mound.

Some of the kingfishers found in Australia and New Guinea have a wide distribution – the sacred kingfisher (*Halcyon sancta*) ranges throughout the Australasian region from New Zealand as far north as the Celebes. The white-collared or mangrove kingfisher (*Halcyon chloris*) is found on the coasts of New Guinea and the northern half of Australia, and also western Pacific islands as far east as Samoa, and north to the coasts of South-East Asia and the Philippines; other populations also occur in western India and the Red Sea. Within this range it shows a considerable amount of variation – some 40 subspecies have been described, a number only exceeded by the golden whistler (described on pages 15 and 18).

Perhaps the most famous of all the Australian kingfishers is the laughing kookaburra (*Dacelo novaeguinae*). As with many birds of remarkable vocal powers, opinions have differed as to the effect the sound has on the human listener – to some 'dawn in the Australian bush has no more delightful or characteristic sound than the chorus of the kookaburras'; but another writer described the laughter as being 'as appalling as the ravings of a madman'.

The kookaburra has now become firmly established as one of Australia's 'national' birds – its laughter is even used as a signature by the Australian Broadcasting Commission. The kookaburras are the largest kingfishers, growing to a length of about 18 inches, with a wing span of nearly two and a half feet; the plumage is among the dullest of any group of kingfishers. Only one of the four species, the rufous-bellied giant kingfisher (*Dacelo gaudichaud*) is found in woods or forest; the other three all prefer open areas, where they feed on a wide variety of large insects, reptiles, crabs, fish, birds, and refuse. They are often common visitors to suburban gardens

Major Mitchell's species is among the most beautiful of the cockatoos, with its white plumage suffused with pink

and take household scraps; they have even adapted to nesting in artificial situations in and around man-made buildings.

The bill of the kookaburra is a massive structure but some other species of kingfisher have even more bizarre bills; the strangest of all is the shovel-billed kingfisher (*Clytoceyx rex*) from New Guinea. In this species the bill, unlike the majority of kingfishers' dagger-like bills, is extremely short and broad. The shape of the bill is undoubtedly connected with the bird's feeding habits; it has been observed (even in old museum specimens) that the bill is often caked in mud, indicating that it is a ground-feeder, grubbing around in the forest litter. The stomach contents also support this, as they include worms, snails, beetles and lizards; other ornithologists also record it as feeding on crabs in mangrove swamps. Another New Guinea species with an unusual bill is the hook-billed kingfisher (*Melidora macrorhina*) which like the previous species appears to be a ground-feeder.

Two birds always associated with Australia are the black swan (*Cygnus atratus*) and the lyrebird (*Menura superba*). The black swan had always been regarded as something quite fabulous and so when the early travellers to Australia brought back tales of these swans, and eventually brought the birds to Europe they were regarded with wonder. The swan is the bird of western Australia, and as such appears on postage stamps and so forth. The lyrebird has also been figured on Australian stamps. It is not spectacularly coloured, but has one of the most beautiful tails found on any of the world's birds, two feathers of the tail forming the arms of the 'lyre' with other finer feathers forming the 'strings'. But the lyrebird possesses other attractions – it has remarkable powers of mimicry. It is not unusual for a lyrebird to imitate the calls of as many as 15 other species of bird, as well as the noise of trains or mechanical saws. The male builds mounds of bare soil on which to display, and performs with his tail spread out over his back.

Of the large flightless birds, the cassowaries (*Casuarius* species) of New Guinea and nearby islands and northern Australia are among the most colourful. There are three species and many geographical races; they have glossy black plumage, a naked blue and red neck and some species have a horny casque and wattles. The rather similar emu (*Dromaius novaehollandiae*) is much dowdier and confined to Australia.

The golden whistler (*Pachycephala pectoralis*) is one of the most interesting examples of geographical variation; not only does the plumage of

The budgerigar is one of the most familiar birds in the world and is now known in many different colours; the wild ancestors of the familiar pet came from the arid interior of Australia and were green and yellow

(Left) only one species of bee-eater is found in Australia, where it is known as the rainbow bird. Here it is shown braking above its nest-hole, with a large dragonfly for its young

(Right) hornbills are widely distributed in Africa and southern Asia, but only one species occurs in New Guinea—the Papuan

the bird vary over its range but also its shape. It is related to the flycatchers, but in many ways looks like a heavily built tit, as it clambers about among forest foliage. The female is a rather drab bird, but the male is boldly marked with olive-green upper parts, a brilliant yellow underside and white throat with blackish head and throat band; the markings of the head and throat show some of the most noticeable geographical varia-tion. The bill shape varies considerably; for example, birds from Tasmania have tiny, stubby bills, those from the Louisiade Archipelago have long slender bills, and those from the Tanimbar Islands have massive shrike-like bills. The interest of this bird to ornithologists is not just the varia-tion that can be observed but rather its distribu-tion. There are over 70 populations sufficiently distinct as to be recognized as subspecies, ranging from Java, east and north to the Moluccas and the islands to the west of New Guinea. It is absent from New Guinea, but reappears on the Bismarck Archipelago, Solomons, New Hebrides and many other islands south and west to Fiji; it also occurs on Tasmania and around the south and west of Australia. Its absence from most of Australia is easily explained by the fact that there is no suitable forest habitat; its absence from New Guinea is not quite so easily explained, the more so since it occurs on nearly all the islands to east and west. It is probably because on the island of New Guinea it is ecologically replaced by the closely related (although dully coloured) grey-headed whistler (*Pachycephala simplex*), which also occurs in the rain forests of Queensland, and on the islands where the golden whistler is absent – in fact, if the distributions of the two species are compared, they fit together like pieces of a jigsaw puzzle. On yet other islands other closely related species occur. A particularly interesting one is the mangrove golden whistler (*Pachycephala melanura*) which looks far more like a 'typical' golden whistler than do many of the latter's variants. The mangrove golden whistler became adapted to living in the coastal mangrove swamps as the climate and vegetation of the interior of Australia deteriorated; once adapted to mangrove swamps it was able to colonize many of the smaller islands and islets which the forest-dwelling golden whistler was unable to colonize. On some of the larger islands and coastal regions the golden whistler's range overlaps that of the mangrove golden whistler and the two, although virtually indistinguishable in the field, do not interbreed, indicating that they are acting as separate species. Just to confuse the picture, on other islands they meet and interbreed to produce very variable hybrid populations. It is just this confusion which interests the professional ornithologist and taxonomist so much, being a living example of the processes of evolution and natural selection at work.

The Solomon Islands have provided several interesting examples of geographical variation apart from the golden whistlers; over the whole group of islands many species have formed recognizably different populations, but the most marked differences are between the populations occurring on San Cristobal and Guadal-canal – which are separated by a mere 20 miles or so. In many cases these two islands are not occupied by just different subspecies but by separate species, the differences being greater than between many of the islands further apart.

Among the prettiest groups of birds endemic to the Australasian region are surely the fairy wrens (Malurinae). The blue wrens (*Malurus* species) must be among the most attractive birds in the world. As in so many birds the female is a fairly dowdy creature, but the male is spectacular; the black-backed wren (*Malurus melanotus*) is almost entirely an iridescent cobalt-blue with just a few bands of black on the rump, the back of the nape and through the eye; the other species are similarly impressive in appearance. But the behaviour of these tiny birds is also fascinating; they are extremely sociable, living in small parties comprising of a pair and a few hangers-on which are apparently adults. During the breeding season each party jointly occupies a nesting territory, defending against intruders. The whole party assists with the task of building, but only the dominant pair produces eggs. After the eggs are laid the 'commune' takes over once again and the whole party helps with the incubation of the eggs and the rearing of the young. This behaviour seems to be a way of ensuring that the brood has a better chance of survival in the extremely harsh conditions found in Australia.

Unlike many of the other large flightless birds such as the ostrich or rhea, the cassowary (left) is not normally found in open country but frequents dense forests

(Left) kingfishers are abundant in the Australasian region though many are found far from water. The species shown here is the little kingfisher from New Guinea

(Right) close-up of the head of a cassowary showing the brilliantly-coloured bare skin and horny casque. Individual populations often vary and in the past many different forms of cassowary were described

The mud-nest builders or magpie-larks (*Grallinidae*) are endemic to the Australasian region, occurring on Australia, Tasmania and New Guinea. They are not particularly striking to look at though one species in particular, the apostle bird (*Struthidea cinerea*), has a fascinating breeding cycle which, like that of the fairy wrens, involves a community of birds. The apostle bird group, which may number up to 17 (though tradition has it that they always go around in dozens – hence the name) all help to build the nest, incubate the eggs and rear the young.

In some cases more than one female lays into the nest, but since it seems that no more than four nestlings can grow up in the nest, there appears to be no advantage in this. Even after the young have left the nest the group continues to feed them for several weeks.

The butcherbirds (Cracticidae) of Australia are completely unrelated to the shrikes (Laniidae) – also known as butcherbirds – but have developed similar behaviour and show some superficial resemblance to the true shrikes in that they make 'larders'. These consist of various items of prey, such as large insects, small reptiles, mammals, birds, etc., which the butcherbird wedges into forks of a tree or impales on thorns of a bush. A close relative of the butcherbirds, the so-called Australian magpie (*Gymnorhina tibicen*) is yet another species which exhibits well developed social behaviour during the breeding season. Unlike some of the other communally-nesting species the Australian magpies do not help with all stages of nesting and rearing of young, but defend a communal territory within which the females build their nest and rear the young alone; there appears to be no pair formation – the birds being promiscuous – but a hierarchy is formed with an older male dominant.

The Australian finches (Estrildidae) are among the most attractive of the small seed-eating birds, and many have become extremely popular with aviculturists. The zebra finch (*Taeniopygia castanotis*) and the Gouldian finches (*Chloebia gouldiae*) are among the most popular. The former has been bred in many colour forms and there is now a wide range which breeds 'true'. The Gouldian finch occurs naturally in three colour forms; the commonest form is grass-green on the back with a blue rump, bright yellow under parts, violet breast, and a red head edged with black and pale blue; the other forms have a black or yellowish-orange head, the latter being extremely rare. Under captive conditions several other colour mutations have also been produced – one of the prettiest being a lutino, still with a red head, but the rest of the body buttercup-yellow.

Black-faced flycatcher bringing food to its mate on the nest. It is found from New Guinea southwards through Eastern Australia to Melbourne

THE ORIENTAL REGION

From the Himalayas to southern China and the islands of South-East Asia

The Oriental region as defined by zoogeographers is that part of Asia lying to the south and east of the Himalayas, extending to the east to meet the Australasian region and meeting the Palearctic to the north and west. Within the region some 1,400 species of birds breed, the most characteristic of which are the pheasants (Phasianidae); it is also rich in woodpeckers (Picidae), cuckoos (Cuculidae) and crows (Corvidae), but because it lacks the physical isolation of most other regions, the Oriental region shows less endemicity.

If one has to pick out a family of birds which could be considered as characteristic of the Oriental region, my choice would immediately fall on the pheasants. There is probably no other group of birds in the Oriental region which can match the pheasants for diversity in structure and plumage. The family Phasianidae includes not only the true pheasants, but also many other birds (often loosely referred to as game-birds) such as snowcocks, francolins, spurfowls, partridges and quails, and the more distantly related subfamilies Tetraoninae (grouse) and Numidinae (guinea-fowl). Of some 48 species of pheasant, all originated in Asia except for the little known Congo peafowl discovered in 1936.

The pheasants have had more effect on man's economic and social history than any other group of birds. Apart from the hunting of the pheasant by the wealthier elements of western society, it must be remembered that the red jungle fowl (*Gallus gallus*) is a pheasant – the ancestor of all the domestic fowl throughout the world and the domestic fowl is the commonest bird in the world. Of the 48 species of pheasant, about one-third are considered to be in danger of extinction in the wild; fortunately pheasants are often reasonably easy to maintain and breed in captivity. The main cause for their decline is undoubtedly the destruction of their habitat coupled with other pressures such as hunting either for food or for their beautiful plumage.

The 48 species of pheasants are grouped into 16 genera – most of which are distinctive. The

Cambodian temple and forest in South-East Asia, one of the most densely populated bird regions in the world

blood pheasant (*Ithnagis cruentus*) is among the most beautiful of all pheasants; it is about the same size and shape as a partridge and the males are delicately coloured bluish-grey above, each feather having a white shaft to the feather, the underside is pale yellowish-green with a crimson throat and undertail coverts, and crimson streaks on the breast – hence the bird's name. There is considerable variation in the plumage of the blood pheasant – up to 13 subspecies are recognized, based mainly on the colour of the male's plumage and the length of the feather 'ears' behind the eye. The blood pheasant lives at higher altitudes than any other species, occurring up to 15,000 feet during the summer and down to about 9,000 feet in winter, in the mountains of Asia, from Tibet and Nepal to western China.

The five species of tragopan or horned pheasant (*Tragopan* species) are among the larger species of pheasant and take their name from the fact that the males are adorned with a pair of bluish lappets and a brilliantly coloured bib which are all inflated during display. Plumage is predominantly in shades of browns, reds and greys with whitish spots. Like the blood pheasant these are mountain birds, but they live at lower altitudes, ranging from about 3,000 feet to 12,000 feet depending on the time of year. At the Pheasant Trust in Norfolk, England, where much work is being done on the conservation of rare pheasants, the following observations on the breeding display of Cabot's tragopan (*T. caboti*) were made. The male begins by standing very upright – so that the body and tail are more or less in a vertical line; the crest is raised and the feathers around the thighs puffed out, then the primaries on the wing nearest the hen are lowered and the shoulder on the opposite side raised – so as to expose as much of the beautifully marked back as possible. In this position the male starts to circle around the female. Suddenly he stops, turns to face the female and the spectacular, if rather grotesque, climax begins. With his plumage fluffed out the male shakes his head until the fleshy horns and the elaborately patterned blue and orange lappet are distended to their full extent; at this point the lappet forms a bib covering the breast. This final part to the display is all over in a matter of a few seconds, and the bird returns to normal.

The monals (*Lophophorus* species) are among the most brilliantly coloured of the pheasants – the iridescence of the male's plumage giving them a really spectacular beauty. Like the previous species the monals are mountain birds living in the Himalayas up to 12,000 feet. Two of the three species known – Sclater's (*L. sclateri*) and the Chinese (*L. lhuysi*) monal – have restricted ranges and are considered to be in danger of extinction if hunting pressures are not reduced. Fortunately the third species, the Himalayan monal (*L. impeyan*), has a much more extensive range and is also being bred in some numbers in captivity.

The ten species included in the genus *Lophura* are rather more varied than those described so far. The genus includes the Kalij and imperial pheasants, the silver pheasant, wattled pheasants, and firebacks. They all have a rather upright stance with a tail which is compressed and ridge-shaped. There are wattles above the eye which are red in all but two species, in which they are blue. They all seem to thrive in captivity and are often seen in zoos and private collections – the most popular probably being the silver pheasant (*Lophura nycthemera*).

The eared pheasants (*Crossoptilon* species) are unique in the group in that the sexes are similar in plumage – all other pheasants have dull coloured females. The eared pheasants take their name from the pair of feathery tufts behind the eye. But the most distinctive feature of the eared pheasants is their tail – it is short, compared with many other species of pheasant, and very deep; the central feathers have the barbs of the feathers only very loosely connected, giving it a lace-like appearance.

The five species of long-tailed pheasants (*Syrmaticus* species) are all being bred in captivity – which is fortunate as they are probably declining in the wild. The story of the mikado pheasant (*S. mikado*) is, however, one of the great successes of the Pheasant Trust; the mikado pheasant was first discovered in 1906 when an ornithologist noticed some tail feathers in the head-dress of a native in their habitat in central Taiwan. In 1912 some were brought to Europe, and in subsequent years between the wars several more pairs were imported into Europe and America; but by the end of World War II the captive stock had dwindled and by the late 1960s there were still only about 25 animals in zoos and a few more in private aviaries. Then the Pheasant Trust obtained some fresh blood from Taiwan, bred 140 young in 1969, and are now pursuing a very successful breeding programme the main aim of which is to

Like most pheasants, the golden species is aggressive and males will often lash out at their rival with their sharp spurs

(Below) the dazzling capes and ruffs of golden pheasants are seen in full glory during display

26

be able to release birds back into the wild.

The pheasants of the genus *Phasianus* are *the* pheasants – including the 'game' pheasant which has been widely introduced throughout the world since Roman times. They show considerable geographical variation in plumage – around 30 subspecies are currently recognized for the common pheasant (*P. colchicus*). The birds living wild in Britain and other parts of Europe are a mixture of various races – the main constituent races being black-necked, ring-necked, green, and Mongolian pheasants.

The most popular of all the 'ornamental' pheasants are the golden (*Chrysolophus pictus*) and Lady Amherst's pheasants (*C. amherstiae*). Their plumage is almost unreal, it is so colourful and elaborate. They are rather smaller than most other species of pheasant and are consequently very popular as cage-birds (as they have been ever since the middle of the 18th century in Britain). Unfortunately, not only do they breed easily but the two species, although extremely dissimilar in appearance, also hybridize very easily. The off-spring are completely fertile, and it is doubtful if any of the captive stock is completely free of hybrid ancestry.

As their name suggests, the peacock pheasants (*Polyplectron* species) look a bit like peacocks and a bit like pheasants. They are birds of dense tropical forest and are rarely seen; the six species

occur from the eastern Himalayas south to Sumatra, Borneo and Palawan. The tail is nothing like as spectacular as that of the peacock, but none the less it is impressive; most species have large eyes, or *ocelli*, on the tail, which is not much longer than the body, and in addition they have numerous smaller *ocelli* on the tail coverts, back and wings. At the culmination of his display the male spreads the tail in a vertical position and lowers the front of the body with the wings spread so as to expose all the colourful markings. The basic colours of the peacock pheasants are shades of browns or greys, the colour of the eyes depending on the species.

Related to the peacock pheasants are the arguses – Rheinart's crested argus (*Rheinartia ocellata*) and the Malay great argus (*Argusianus argus*). The former has the distinction of possessing the largest tail feathers of all the world's birds. Both species are polygamous; the male clears a display arena in an open part of the forest which he keeps free of leaves and other obstructions, and in this arena performs his elaborate 'dance'. The male great argus, apart from its size, is not outstanding in its plumage except for its enormous secondaries which extend nearly half the length of the tail and are marked with *ocelli*. As soon as a female enters the male's arena he starts to display; he takes up a position facing her, bends forward and spreads his wings

28

*(Left) crimson horned
pheasant. The pheasant
family is characteristic
of India and the
Oriental region; all the
known species occur
within that area.
Unfortunately several
species have declined as
a result of man's
destruction of their
habitat, or from hunting
pressures*

over his head so that the outer primaries meet and touch the ground. The inner secondaries meet over his back and his tail projects over them. The beautiful *ocelli* are now displayed to full advantage – occasionally the male adds a finishing touch by vibrating his body so that the *ocelli* appear to revolve. If his courtship is successful, once the birds have mated then the female will go off to lay her eggs and rear the young without any further assistance from the male. He will try and seduce another passing hen.

The peafowl are probably one of the best known of the 'ornamental' pheasants – they have been kept in parks and gardens since ancient times. Contrary to popular belief the long train of the male is not in fact his tail, but the tail coverts; the tail is a much shorter and stiffer affair used to support the train. There are two species of peafowl (*Pavo* species) and additionally the closely-related Congo peacock (*Afropavo congensis*). The Indian peafowl (*Pavo cristatus*) and green peafowl (*P. muticus*) are so well known as not to need any description. The Congo peafowl on the other hand is one of the least known birds in the world. It was not known to science until 1936 when an American ornithologist noticed two stuffed specimens in the Congo Museum* in Belgium, and realized that it was a previously undescribed species. He was able to procure fresh specimens from the Congo, and in the period 1959–1962 Antwerp Zoo obtained live animals from which they were able to produce a brood of three young in 1964. A peacock without a train is the best way of describing this bird's appearance.

The Far East is the home of what must surely be the most spectacularly colourful duck in the world – the mandarin duck (*Aix galericulata*). Strictly speaking these birds are outside the scope of this book as they breed in the temperate parts of Manchuria and Japan, but they winter south as far south as Tonkin. They have been taken to many parts of the world and, like the closely related and equally beautiful North American wood duck or Carolina duck (*Aix sponsa*), they have become popular in parks and zoos, and have also established free-living (feral) populations in many parts of the world.

Although not confined exclusively to tropical regions, flamingoes (Phoenicopteridae) are among the groups of birds which are usually associated with the tropics. Indeed they occur on all continents except Australia (in fact they are absent from the whole of Australasia, and most of eastern Asia). There are four species, the most

*Since 1971 the area south of the Congo river is called Zaire, and the Congo Museum has been renamed the *Musée royal de l'Afrique centrale*.

Blue eared pheasant. The illustrations on pages 26–37 give an idea of the diversity of this usually colourful group (only males are shown)

31

widespread of which is the greater flamingo (*Phoenicopterus ruber*) which has a number of well differentiated populations, one of which, from South America, is often regarded as a full species – *P. chilensis*. The greater flamingo occurs in northern South America, the Caribbean, eastern and southern Africa, India and Central Asia, and around the Mediterranean; the *chilensis* populations occur in southern South America. The actual number of breeding sites of all species of flamingo is fairly small, but outside the breeding season they often spread out over a very wide area. Apart from their spectacular coloration, flamingoes have a fascinating appearance; their bizarre form has attracted ornithologist and layman alike – to Lewis Carroll their peculiar angled beaks seemed more suitable for use as croquet mallets than as food-gatherers. The entire world population has been estimated at somewhere in the region of a million birds, that of the African and Indian populations (*P.r. roseus*) being about 600,000 of which the greatest number nest in the Rann of Kutch in Baluchistan. Also in this area is the lesser flamingo (*Phoeniconaias minor*), most of whose world population is in Africa.

The hornbills (Bucerotidae) of India and South-East Asia, like their African relatives, show superficial similarity to the toucans (Ramphasti-

dae) of South America. Like the toucans the Asian hornbills are largely forest-dwellers and have not moved into open country to the extent that their African relatives have. The most spectacular of the Asian hornbills is the great hornbill (*Buceros bicornis*) which grows to a length of nearly five feet. Its plumage is mainly black, with white patches on wings and tail and a white neck; the white usually becomes stained yellowish by a greasy secretion from the preen gland. In life the massive bill and casque is a deep yellow, but this fades in dead animals and often in captives – although if they are fed with foods which contain an abundance of yellow or orange pigments they keep their colour better.

One of the strangest commodities man has ever traded in is surely hornbill 'ivory'. This is made from one species only – the helmeted hornbill (*Rhinoplax vigil*) – not from the bill which is light and cellular, but the casque surmounting the bill which is dense and suitable for carving. It is only found in Malaya, Sumatra, and Borneo and most of the ivory is thought to have originated in Borneo. The ivory was not worked in Borneo but exported to China where an idea of its value can be gained from the fact that elephant ivory cost only half as much. The ivory was carved into a variety of forms including figurines,

belt clasps and also snuff-boxes. But the most impressive work of all is in the form of whole heads in which the casque is carved with an ornamental scene and the head covered with the feathers of peacocks and other birds.

Unfortunately the technique of the craftsmen is completely lost and very few examples of hornbill ivory are known – only half a dozen complete casques have been found.

The cuckoos are cosmopolitan in their distribution, but some of the most striking and colourful members of the family are to be found in south-eastern Asia. Unlike the familiar cuckoo of Europe, many species do not parasitize other birds, but make their own nest and rear their own young. Amongst these are the six malcohas (*Phaenicophaeus* species) which are found in an area centred around the Malay Peninsula. They are colourful birds with fairly long, graduated tails and richly coloured plumage – usually reds, purples, browns and iridescent blues and greens; the most striking feature, however, is the brightly coloured patch of bare skin, around the eye, which is usually blue or red. Perhaps the strangest of all the cuckoo family are the 25 members of the genus *Centropus*, known as coucals. The common coucal (*C. sinensis*) which is found throughout India and South-East Asia, has also been called the 'crow pheasant' as it looks quite like both these species, and is also known as the 'subaltern's pheasant' – presumably young officers in India shot the bird in mistake for a true pheasant. Another species, from Australia, the pheasant coucal (*C. phasianus*) looks even more like a female pheasant. The common coucal is a large bird – some 20 inches long with large rounded wings, long tail, glossy black body and tail plumage and rich brown wings.

A family of birds which probably has its centre of radiation in South-East Asia is the Pittidae. The pittas, or jewel thrushes as they have occasionally been known, are thought to be related to the New World's passerines in the order Tyanni; however, of the 23 species only three extend outside South-East Asia to Australia, and another two are confined to Africa.

Although the variety of colour found within the family is dazzling, in other respects they are remarkably similar in structure and overall shape – so similar in fact that they are all classified in one genus, *Pitta*. One of the largest, most widespread, and best known species is the blue-winged pitta (*Pitta moluccensis*). It is nearly eight inches long, with the typical dumpy appearance of the pitta – rather like a thrush that has lost its tail. The underside is a warm, buff colour, the back green with bright blue on the wings; the crown is brown

(Left) mikado pheasant

Elliot's pheasant

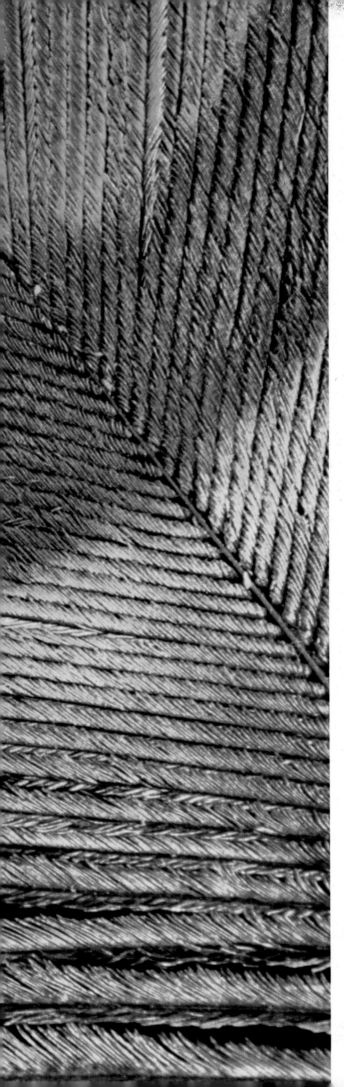

and the sides of the head and nape black. Like the other pittas they are ground-dwellers living amongst the litter on the forest floor, feeding on berries, insects, worms and any other small animals. They are easily overlooked, on account of their skulking habits, but will often give their presence away by their loud whistles. Although they are strong fliers, they usually avoid taking to the wing and instead move around with enormous kangaroo-like leaps and bounds. Most species of pitta are about six to eight inches long, though one species, the giant pitta (*Pitta caerulea*) grows to 11 inches. It is almost impossible to describe the variety of colour found in this small group. Some seem to have all the colours of the rainbow in their plumage. Among the most beautiful is the garnet pitta (*P. granatina*) which is black, with a purplish sheen above the blood red below; behind its eye is a long, tapering and whitish eye-stripe.

Although the trogons (Trogonidae) are mainly found in Africa and in South America, one genus, *Harpactes*, is confined to South-East Asia. They show some slight resemblance to the South American trogons of the genus *Trogon*.

Several of the 11 species, such as the orange-breasted trogon (*Harpactes oreskios*), are widespread while some, such as Whitehead's trogon, are confined to limited areas. Although they are so distinct a family, they show remarkable uniformity within the family. One of the most distinctive trogon features is the structure of their toes – two pointing forward and two pointing back (as with woodpeckers, cuckoos and parrots among other groups, but unlike these birds the trogons have the second toe pointing back instead of the fourth). In plumage the *Harpactes* trogons are very similar – delicate pinks and browns often with dark throat and breast. But the most distinctive character of the plumage is not its colour but its texture – extremely soft and fluffy, and the skin to which the plumage is attached is paper-thin, making it very difficult to prepare museum skins.

Considerably smaller than the trogons are the barbets (Capitonidae), a family that is widespread in the tropical regions, particularly south-eastern Asia. Like the woodpeckers to which they are fairly closely related, they have two toes pointing forward and two back, but the woodpeckers are mainly insect-eaters whereas the barbets feed mainly on fruits, berries, seeds, buds and even nectar. They spend most of their life in the canopy of the forest and are more often heard than seen. Many of them have very distinctive, if rather monotonous, calls which can be heard for hour after hour. The coppersmith barbet (*Megalaima haemacephala*), for instance, takes its name from

Eyed feather from the train of an Indian peafowl

39

its ringing call notes which sound like a hammer striking an anvil.

The plumage of many of the barbets makes them very difficult to pick out in the forest canopy – the *Megalaima* barbets have a leaf-green body and differ mainly in the head markings. The many-coloured barbet (*M. rafflesi*), which occurs from Malaya to Sumatra and Borneo is spectacularly marked, with a red crown, blue throat, and with patches of blue, red, black, yellow and orange on the sides of the head and around the eye.

The drongos (Dicruridae) are a family of passerines more or less confined to South-East Asia – of the 20 species only three occur in Africa, one is confined to mountains of New Guinea and the rest are more or less Oriental in their distribution. They nearly all have black plumage which contrasts with areas of iridescent feathers – blue, green or purple depending on the species. They

The magnificent 'tail' of the peacock is in reality its tail coverts – the short, stiff tail merely supports the magnificent train during display

Cuckoos are widespread
in the Oriental region,
though many of them
are not parasitic, as is
the familiar European
species. Shown here is
the white-browed coucal

are aggressive birds and although mostly under about ten inches, they will attack and drive away any larger birds such as crows which try to interfere with them. Although they are probably related to the flycatchers, in their ecology they are most similar to the shrikes. The tail shape of several species is impressive; the racquet-tailed drongo (*Dicrurus paradiseus*), for instance, not only has extremely long outer tail feathers but has the webbing worn away down most of the length

so as to form the racquets at the end – these tail feathers are often over 15 inches long. Others such as the black drongo (*Dicrurus macrocercus*) have a deep outward-sweeping fork to the tail.

Often occurring in similar habitats to the drongos are the mynahs. These birds form part of the starling family (Sturnidae) and are nearly all found in the Oriental region. The most famous of all is the Indian hill mynah (*Gracula religiosa*), known mainly for its superlative

Rothschild's mynah (starling or grackle as it is variously known) is confined to a small area of Bali, and although protected many birds are smuggled out for the pet trade

powers of imitating human speech. It is often considered an 'ideal' cage-bird both in the countries where it is found and in the developed countries. Unfortunately the tremendous demand that Britain, other European countries and America have created for this bird is leading to a substantial reduction of their numbers in the wild. Just how many mynahs are involved in the pet trade is not known, but Thailand recently restricted their export to 60,000 a year; equivalent figures for other parts of their range can only be guessed at. Since it is the young birds which make the best talkers there is a great demand for the nestlings or 'gapers' as they are known.

The way they are collected only helps to accelerate the decline of the species – mynahs nest in holes in trees and the trees are often cut down in order to get at the nests, thereby destroying future potential nest sites. Many visitors to Thailand and other parts of the mynah's range have remarked that outside the national parks and other protected areas, the mynah is becoming increasingly rare or has even disappeared; the blame for this can largely be laid on the pet dealers and keepers of the western world. How many of the owners of mynahs would be prepared to give £10 to £15 towards conservation – the amount they probably paid for their pet bird?

On the island of Bali lives the rarest of all mynahs – variously known as Rothschild's mynah, starling, or grackle (*Leucopsar rothschildi*). This beautiful bird is white, with the tips of the wings and tail black and a white, drooping crest; the skin around the eye is bare and bright blue in colour. Rothschild's mynah is confined to a very limited area in Bali and has suffered in the past from collectors for the pet trade. The Indonesian government have afforded the species full protection, but unfortunately it can still be imported into Britain and many other countries, even though it may have been smuggled illegally from Bali where it is difficult to enforce an export ban of this nature. Recently several aviculturists have bred this species and, as the colonies become well established, it should be possible to breed enough to satisfy the demand from the pet trade and so remove the pressure on the wild birds.

Another species of mynah, the common mynah (*Acridotheres tristis*), can claim to be one of the most widely introduced species. From its native South-East Asia it has been exported to Australia, New Zealand, many islands in the Pacific and Indian Oceans, southern Africa and Madagascar. The closely related Chinese jungle mynah (*Acridotheres cristatellus*) has also been introduced into the area around Vancouver in Canada.

Although by no means confined to the Oriental

Brahminy kite, a familiar sight in many parts of India. It may even be seen scavenging over cities

Indian coursers, like their relatives from other regions, are supremely adapted for desert conditions. Here the bird is settling on eggs which a few feet away would be almost impossible to distinguish from the stony ground on which they are laid

43

region the crows (Corvidae) are fairly character-istic of the area, many species being strikingly beautiful. The typical crows (*Corvus*) are not particularly abundant, though the ubiquitous house crow (*Corvus splendens*) has the unique distinction of being the only bird which is always associated with man throughout its range.

It is the colourful magpies, jays and tree-pies for which the Oriental region is just famous. Most of the species bear a superficial resemblance to the jays and magpies found in Europe and North America, but are even more colourful. The green magpies (*Cissa* species), for instance, are basically emerald-green with a slight crest at the back of the head; the bill is blood-red and a black streak extends from the bill back through the eye. The wings are deep rufous with prominent white spots. The tail is graduated as in most other species of magpie, but the short-tailed green magpie (*Cissa thalassina*) as its name implies does not have a very long tail. Probably the most beautiful of all are the five species of blue magpie (*Urocissa*), the most familiar of which is the red-billed magpie (*U. erythrorhyncha*), sometimes seen in zoos and private collections. The plumage

of this species is mainly pale blue, and on wings and tail, black, grey and white, offset by a bright red bill and feet; but it is the graduated tail which is the outstanding feature – it is over twice the length of the bird's body and each of the powder-blue feathers is banded with black, then white at the tip, except the longest (central) pair which are tipped with white alone.

To ornithologists the azure-winged magpie (*Cyanopica cyana*) is one of the enigmas of the bird world. In appearance it is pretty, but not outstandingly beautiful – it is its distribution which is so puzzling to ornithologists. It occurs in the Far East and then after a gap reappears in western Spain and Portugal; the main difference between the two populations is that the eastern birds have white tips to the tail feathers.

What caused this strange distribution is not entirely certain but it is probable that the species used to have a more extensive range and the two populations were once linked; since that time the species range has been receding. There is evidence that its range is still declining as there are many suitable areas within, or close to, its present-day range from which it is absent.

THE ETHIOPIAN REGION

Africa, south of the Sahara and including Madagascar

Of the tropical regions of the world it is probably Africa which is the most familiar – and many of its birds are also familiar, either through films, zoos, or even through travel; Africa is now very much on the map as far as tourism is concerned.

The Ethiopian region is the term used by zoogeographers to denote the continent of Africa – though it excludes Africa north of the Sahara (considered to be faunistically part of Europe) and includes a corner of Arabia; Madagascar is also included and forms a subregion. Altogether it comprises an area of nearly 11,500,000 square miles, of which nearly 80 per cent occurs within the tropics. But whereas the Neotropical region has over 30 per cent of the land covered by tropical rain forest, Africa has less than 10 per cent; and whereas South America has only around 3 per cent of its area classifiable as desert, Africa has nearly 30 per cent. It is this difference in available habitat which largely accounts for the fact that Africa, though much larger, has only some 1,600 species of birds compared with South America's 2,500.

The birds characteristic of the Ethiopian region include the guinea-fowl (Numidinae), the secretary bird (Sagittariidae), the vultures (Aegypidiidae), ostrich (Struthionidae), bald crows (Picathartinae), weavers (Ploceidae); many of these groups share some of their species with the Palearctic region or even the Oriental region. Other groups which, although not confined to Africa, show considerable diversity within that continent include larks (Alaudidae), shrikes (Laniidae), bustards (Otidae), hornbills (Bucerotidae) and bee-eaters (Meropidae).

The birds found in desert regions tend to be few and far between and many of them are cryptically coloured and so rather unspectacular to look at. Some of them show remarkable adaptations to the rigours of desert life.

Sandgrouse (Pteroclidae) are one of the characteristic birds of dry areas in both Africa and Asia. They are able to survive in extremely arid habitats where few other birds can tolerate the harsh conditions. Sandgrouse, thought to be related to pigeons, have somewhat pigeon-like heads and plumpish bodies. Most species have a rather long, tapering tail and fairly long, pointed wings. The feet are set well forward on the body, making them rather awkward on the ground; once on the wing they are, however, strong and swift fliers. Sandgrouse are always dependent on a supply of water and in some species, particularly those living in arid conditions, they may congregate around water-holes, gathering in flocks numbering several thousands. As they gather, some birds which cannot find space around the water-holes settle on the surface of the water to drink – they are able to float well and take off again quite easily when they have finished. It is possible that this habit of actually settling on the surface of the water has led to one of the most interesting behavioural patterns to have been discovered in sandgrouse. It has been observed that when the male has finished drinking he crouches in the shallows and thoroughly soaks the feathers on his belly. When he returns to the chicks – which cannot, of course, fly to the water-hole – they gather under him and 'milk' him of the moisture he has brought them by stripping the sodden feathers through their beaks.

The feathers are modified for this function and have highly specialized barbules which can contain much more water than a normal feather – for instance the belly feathers of the male namaqua sandgrouse (*Pterocles namaqua*) can carry between 15 and 20 times the bird's weight in water; ordinary feathers will not hold much more than five or six times the bird's weight.

Just as there are a variety of large mammals characteristic of the plains of Africa, so there are some large birds, the largest of which is the ostrich (*Struthio camelus*). It is, in fact, the largest living bird but is flightless; its wings are reduced to mere sprouts of feathers, but the long muscular legs enable the ostrich to sprint at speeds of up to 40 mph. Their toes have been reduced to two in number and are almost hoof-like – a kick from an ostrich can inflict a nasty wound on almost any would-be predator. Another adaptation of the

The Ngorongoro Crater —a typical view of the East African plains

47

ostrich to its environment is its long neck which enables it to see far across the plains. Because the feathers are no longer needed for flight the barbs which normally keep a feather in shape have degenerated, and ostrich feathers are soft and loose. The wing and tail feathers of the male are used in display and it is these feathers which are used by the fashion trade. Although no longer as popular as they used to be, ostriches are still farmed for their plumes in South Africa (and also in South America and Australia).

Of the 21 species of bustard (Otidae) 14 are basically African. The largest species occur in India and the Palearctic region and are among the heaviest flying birds in the world – weighing up to 40 lb; all the bustards found in Africa are also fairly large birds.

Bustards are not particularly conspicuously marked – in fact they tend to have cryptic colora-tion, particularly the females. However, a displaying male is a spectacular sight revealing plumage of undreamed-of splendour; in most species the head is thrown back as he puffs out his chest, and his wings and tail are raised until it is almost impossible to recognize him as a bird at all.

Like the ostrich, bustards have a relatively long neck, and long powerful legs. Although they are strong fliers they often rely on their running ability to escape danger. As they methodically pick their way across the plains looking for locusts, lizards and similar prey they disturb many other insects from the vegetation; another group of birds uses this habit to advantage – the bee-eaters (Meropidae), which will often perch on the bustard's back and hawk for the insects.

Of the 24 species of bee-eaters over two-thirds breed in Africa. They are among the most colourful birds in the world – and the most

Carmine bee-eaters around their nest burrows in a sandy bank. The brilliant pink plumage of these birds makes the sight of a large colony, which may number several thousands, a dazzling spectacle

*Portrait of a
red-throated bee-eater*

spectacular of all is perhaps the carmine bee-eater (*Merops nubicus*). Not only does its brilliant plumage give a dazzling effect, but it often nests in very large colonies exceeding a thousand or more birds; a colony of this size is almost overwhelming in its beauty. Most bee-eaters are colonial nesters, excavating nest tunnels either in a cliff or, in certain species, into level ground;

these tunnels may be anything up to nine feet long. All the African bee-eaters have a rather similar basic shape; most species are around eight to ten inches long, the smallest being six inches and the largest about 14 inches long; they all have fairly strong, slender and slightly decurved bills. In many species the central tail feathers extend beyond the rest of the tail but in

(Left) male carmine bee-eater in flight, showing the elongated central tail feathers characteristic of most species of bee-eater

(Right) chestnut-bellied sandgrouse at a water hole. Often vast numbers gather together and those which cannot reach the water's edge settle on the surface to drink while floating

(Right) four-banded sandgrouse drinking. The males soak their breast and belly feathers in the water and then return to their young, which may be far from water, to give the chicks a drink

(Left) carmine bee-eater perched on the back of a kori bustard, from whence it will make short sallies to catch any insects the bustard disturbs as it strides across the plains

Group of young ostriches. These large, flightless birds were once found not only in South and East Africa but also in North Africa and the Middle East

Male kori bustard puffed up in courtship display. Bustards are characteristic of the open plains, and even semi-desert regions

one species, the swallow-tailed bee-eater (*Merops hirundineus*), the tail is deeply forked.

The main differences between the species are the colours which quite literally include all those of the rainbow. As their name implies, they feed to a large extent on Hymenoptera, honey-bees being a particular favourite with many species; they also take various other insects, particularly Orthoptera, such as grasshoppers, locusts, and crickets, which are often flushed by bush fires. Bee-eaters, along with kites, rollers and various other birds are frequently attracted to the edges of bush fires where they prey on the fleeing insects.

Pelicans (Pelicanidae) have a rather primeval look about them – like some kind of pterodactyl – and indeed they are known from fossils dating back about 40,000,000 years; these fossils are virtually indistinguishable from living forms. The seven species of pelican occur throughout the world, though they are mainly found in the warmer regions. Throughout most of the world they tend to have rather patchy distribution – undoubtedly they were once more widespread, but availability of suitable habitat must also be an important factor governing their distribution. Certainly their decrease in Europe, for instance, is largely as a result of habitat destruction and

human interference. All seven species of the world's pelicans are very similar in appearance – the most obvious differences being in coloration.

In Africa two species occur, the white pelican (*Pelicanus onocrotalus*) and the pink-backed pelican (*P. rufescens*). Like the other species they are large, rather ungainly-looking birds on land, but superbly adapted to their environment. They are up to five feet long and may have a wing span of anything up to nine feet; once in the air they are great fliers. They are sociable at all times, even gathering together to feed; they drive fish into shallow water where they scoop them up in their enormous throat pouches. It is their sociability which has in many ways accelerated their rapid decline by making them an easy target for hunters. During the breeding season their nests and young are also extremely vulnerable to predators, the more so since the parents desert fairly easily when disturbed. Many of the lakes which have large pelican populations, particularly those in the East-African Rift Valley, also have sizable flamingo populations.

Only two species of flamingo are found in Africa – the greater flamingo (*Phoenicopterus ruber*) and the lesser flamingo (*Phoeniconaias minor*). Although the greater flamingo is more widely distributed, it is the lesser species which is the more abundant in Africa – in fact most of the lesser flamingo population is confined to a few breeding sites in eastern and southern Africa. Around 3,000,000 birds – about two-thirds of the world population – breed around the Rift Valley lakes.

The flamingo family is adapted to feeding in shallow, brackish water, filtering particles from the water or bottom mud. Lesser flamingoes feed entirely on algae which they gather as they wade through the water sweeping their bills from side to side. The bill, as in all flamingoes, is modified for this action, and is bent down so that it can sweep the water when the head is upside-down; the bill contains fine laminae through which water is pumped by the action of the tongue, and the fine particles are filtered out – an action comparable to that of the baleen whales. Lesser flamingoes are the only large birds which feed on the blue-green algae of the East African soda lakes – and they are able to concentrate there in enormous numbers.

Remarkably enough the main breeding grounds for the lesser flamingoes were unknown until comparatively recent times; in 1954 the ornithologist Leslie Brown discovered a flock of about 500,000 pairs nesting on Lake Natron,

only 100 miles from Nairobi. This lake has partly dried up and the enormous deposits of sodium carbonate are covered with a thick black mud. Although the flamingoes are visible from the air, from the shore of the lake the vast majority of the birds are completely hidden from view by the heat haze. The local Masai believe that the young emerge from the waters of the lake fully developed – this is because the young do not appear around the edges of the lake until they are almost fully grown, spending the previous weeks around the open waters far across the mud and soda. By nesting in these extreme conditions the lesser flamingoes are safe from practically all large predators, man included. Other famous localities for seeing lesser flamingoes are Lake Nakuru and Lake Hannington where as many as 2,000,000 have been recorded.

One of the most distinctive groups of larger birds, common in most of the open woodlands and scrub areas of tropical Africa is the hornbill family (Bucerotidae). Although by no means confined to Africa – many species occur from India through to South-East Asia – it is the African species which have been most studied. One of the commonest and most widespread of the smaller hornbills (*Tockus* species) is the African red-billed hornbill (*T. erythrorhychus*),

(Above) flock of lesser flamingoes seen from a distance; these flocks on the East African soda lakes are often vast, numbering many thousands of birds

(Right) some of the larger birds characteristic of Lake Nakuru. Lesser flamingoes, white pelicans, terns and various ducks can be picked out

Unique shot of an African hoopoe hovering in front of its nestling while feeding it. These birds are characteristic of drier habitats and even occur well into Europe

but others such as the African grey hornbill (*T. nasutus*), the yellow-billed hornbill, and Von der Decken's hornbill (*T. deckeni*) are also often to be found in the same habitat of open savannah and thornbush; other species in the genus are forest-dwellers.

Superficially these small hornbills resemble the aracaris and toucanets of the South American forests, and the larger hornbills show a striking resemblance to the toucans; the structure of the bill is remarkably similar – though the toucans always lack the casque which is sometimes found atop the hornbill's bill. The toucans, toucanets, and aracaris, are almost exclusively forest-dwellers whereas the hornbills are found in a wide variety of other habitats.

The small *Tockus* hornbills are fairly gregarious and are often to be seen in small parties; they are

remarkably strong and graceful fliers for such ungainly-looking birds. In a sort of follow-my-leader procession they flap from tree to tree in family parties in search of food. Their diet is very varied – largely depending on the season – they feed on a wide variety of seeds, berries and fruits (especially figs) as well as insects, lizards and eggs, and young of other birds. Insects, lizards, and any other small animals are often sought out along the edges of bush fires when the hornbills will capture them as they flee the flames. But the most interesting aspect of the hornbill's life is its breeding behaviour which, as far as is known, is roughly similar in most species.

All the *Tockus* hornbills breed in large holes in trees, or occasionally cracks in rocks or cliffs, preferably with a constricted entrance. The parent birds set about reducing the size of the

Greater flamingoes, from Africa, some tending their young, others performing territorial displays

entrance hole by plastering it with a mixture of mud and saliva; when the hole is reduced to such a size that the birds can only just get in and out of the nest, the female enters the chamber and assists from the inside using the mud brought by the male mixed with dung and saliva as well as any wood chips and other debris which may be around. The flat sides of the hornbill's bill are used to smooth the 'cement'. Gradually the female is walled in, until only a narrow slit remains, and then on a pile of wood chips and other rotting debris she lays from three to six pale eggs. Whilst incarcerated in the nest chamber the female is fed by the male, and she undergoes a moult; the tail feathers are moulted first, then the wing feathers, rendering her completely flightless for a short period. When the eggs have hatched the male has to feed the entire brood on

(Left) pink-backed pelican taking off. Although rather ungainly-looking birds, once they have managed the difficult task of becoming airborne, pelicans are remarkably strong fliers

(Right) young pink-backed pelican swallowing a fish. The enormous throat pouch is used to scoop up fish

his own. By the time the chicks are about half-grown the female has regrown her wing feathers and she breaks out from her prison – by now it is often very crowded and quite fetid. Once the female has left the nest the young perform what is perhaps the most remarkable part of the whole nesting cycle – they plaster up the entrance slit from the inside. The instinct to do this appears to exist only at a certain stage, and it is usually the eldest of the chicks which perform the operation. The female may spend around two and a half months sealed in the nest chamber, and then the young up to another month after she has left; in some other groups of hornbills the mother emerges at the same time as her offspring.

Birds of prey occur in all regions of the world, but it is probably in Africa that they are most apparent. Few species except the rarely-seen owls and the falcons are normally considered as particularly attractive birds. In fact the usual reaction to vultures is one of revulsion. And yet the vultures are superbly adapted for performing what is a very important task – that of cleaning up the countryside. The eagle commands respect for its regal magnificence, but the poor vultures are spurned. Most vultures feed on carrion and in order to stop themselves becoming fouled with gore, they have evolved almost naked heads and necks; the neck is also long to enable the vulture to feed in all the cavities of a large mammalian carcass. One of the species of vulture which has a completely feathered head is the bearded vulture or lammergeier (*Gypaetus barbatus*), once widespread even in southern Europe. This species is a scavenger, but has also evolved a most interesting piece of behaviour: it carries large bones and skulls to a rocky area and drops them from a height of up to 200 feet to break them open; it then extracts the marrow and eats the bone fragments. The gut is modified to digest bone.

Although by no means exclusively Ethiopian in their distribution, the shrikes (Laniidae) are particularly well represented and diverse in Africa. One of the most fascinating groups is the bush shrike belonging to the genera *Telophorus* and *Malaconotus*. In this group there may be more variation within a particular species than between it and another species. For instance the many-coloured bush shrike (*Telophorus multicolor*) may be bright red beneath, or lemon-yellow, or have a blue-black throat and breast, with orange-yellow below. But it is only the *Telephorus* bush shrikes which exhibit this polymorphism – each species of *Malaconotus* bush shrike occurs only in a single colour phase but this is often very similar to one of the colour phases of *Telophorus*.

Mixed flock of vultures squabbling over the carcass of a young hartebeeste; among the scavenging animals there is normally a strict hierarchy around a carcass

Another genus of African shrikes, *Laniarius*, includes the ten bush shrikes known as boubous and gonaleks. Their plumages are also diverse, and in many cases quite beautiful, with brightly-coloured red or yellow under parts contrasting with black or slaty upper parts. Unlike most other groups of shrikes they do not hunt from an exposed perch, but spend most of their time hunting in dense bushes. But the point of particular interest in this group is their song – each pair of birds performs a duet. Duetting is known from several groups of tropical birds, but the duets of the bush shrikes are particularly well developed and have been studied in some detail. One of the commonest calls, made by several species is 'boubou', but each pair has its own particular repertoire of calls and replies which are usually uttered from positions about ten yards apart, though sometimes they may be separated by over 100 yards. The unrelated brubru (*Nilaus afer*) is another shrike found in southern Africa which performs a rather similar duet to the boubous.

The helmet shrikes (*Prionops* species) are sufficiently different from other shrikes to be regarded by some taxonomists as forming a separate family. There are seven species altogether, but three have very restricted ranges. They are predominantly grey birds with varying amounts of black and white, the only really bright colour being on the feet and bill, or around the eye-ring. Unlike the true shrikes, which are pugnacious little predators, the helmet shrikes are on the whole inoffensive, feeding mainly on small insects and their grubs. Their nests are quite unlike those of any other species of shrike, being constructed from mosses, lichens, grasses and other fine vegetation held together with spiders' webs and well concealed among foliage.

The bald crows which form a subfamily (Picathartinae) within the babblers are a strange group found in isolated colonies in the vast forests of West Africa. The two species are both about the size of a large thrush with dark grey plumage above and whitish below; the head is devoid of feathering and in the grey-necked bald crow (*Picathartes oreas*) the skin is blue, black, and red, and in the white-necked species (*P. gymnocephalus*) it is black and yellow. Both species live in and around caves, feeding on lizards, snakes, insects and other invertebrates which are found among the bat dung and other detritus on the floor of the cave.

The waxbills (Estrildidae) are a family of small seed-eating birds found in Africa, Asia and Australia, but the greatest variety of species occurs in Africa. They are attractive little birds

and popular as cage-birds – vast numbers are exported from Africa to satisfy the pet trade.

Species such as the orange-cheeked waxbill (*Estrilda melpoda*) the red-eared waxbill (*E. trogolodytes*), the lavender finch (*E. caerulescens*), the cordon bleus (*Uraeginthus* species) are all a familiar sight in pet shops.

The five species which comprise the genus *Uraeginthus* are among the prettiest of the waxbills. The genus can be divided into two groups; the cordon bleus, which have a large amount of blue in the plumage and the grenadiers, which have purple in the plumage. They exhibit behaviour typical of many waxbills. The most frequently seen display is that known as the 'straw display' in which the male collects a small piece of straw or grass and flies to a perch, calling as he flies; he then approaches the hen, or she may come to him; the male then bobs up and

down and begins to sing his squeaky little song.

The nest built by the waxbills gives rise to their alternative name of 'weaver finches' – though this name leads to confusion with the true weavers (Ploceidae) – they build loosely woven nests of a wide variety of shapes. The *Estrilda* species build the most elaborate ones and close by they also build a nest known as the 'cock nest'. Various species of birds build such nests and at one time it was commonly believed that the cocks used them to roost in. In the waxbills this is certainly not their function; it is more likely that the nest is to confuse potential predators. When the birds are disturbed, they fly in and out of the cock nest in an ostentatious manner, whereas when they enter the real nest it is usually done unobtrusively and quickly, without fuss.

The whydahs (*Vidua* species) are members of the weaver family which are brood parasites of

Malachite kingfisher, brilliant even in a family renowned for dazzling colours

D'Arnaud's barbet about to take a beakful of insect food to its young, which are in the nest burrow behind it

the waxbills. In appearance some of the whydahs are remarkably similar to each other but parasitize different species of waxbill – for instance the range of Fischer's whydah (*Vidua fischeri*) covers almost exactly the same area as that of the purple grenadier, the species which is its host in eastern Africa; similarly in southern Africa the shaft-tailed whydah (*V. regia*) has a distribution which closely matches that of its host, the common grenadier. Unfortunately the relationship of host and parasite is, in some cases, much more complicated; also the fact that apparently a single species can be divided on the grounds that it parasitizes more than one species has led some ornithologists to suggest that the normal concept of species, as applied to other bird species, may not be acceptable for a group as complicated as the whydahs.

Among the remarkable features of the waxbills are the conspicuous, bright patterns which the young have on the inside of the mouth. When these are shown to the parents they stimulate the parent bird into regurgitating food for the young. The whydahs, in order to be fed by their hosts have mimicked these markings in incredible detail. Unlike some cuckoos and other brood parasites the whydah's young do not eject the other eggs or young from the nest, but have to compete with their waxbill nest-mates.

The rest of the birds comprizing the weaver family are grouped in a separate subfamily to the whydahs, and include the familiar house sparrow beautiful bishop bird, and infamous queleas.

The red-billed quelea (*Quelea quelea*) is found in most of the savannah and dry, open country of Africa south of the Sahara. It breeds in dense colonies usually near a water source.

The nests are built entirely by the males, just before the females arrive at the colony. It has been estimated that an average-sized colony may contain around 500,000 nests – a single tree may contain over 5,000. Large colonies contain 10,000,000 or more birds, and ornithologists studying them near Lake Chad found colonies of this sort of size every few miles along the shores of the lake. The breeding cycle is very rapid indeed; after spending a couple of days building the nest the eggs only take about 14 days to hatch and the young have left the nest after only another 14 days; all the activities are closely synchronized throughout the colony.

Obviously colonies the size of the quelea's are going to consume a considerable quantity of food and since the enormous flocks often descend on man's cereal crops they are considered a pest over most parts of their range – in fact they are often known as 'locust birds'. The task of

The cordon bleu waxbill is among the most popular of this group, in a family of birds which is a favourite of many aviculturists

controlling quelea numbers is hampered by the fact that most of the colonies are found far from cultivated lands and do not rely on crops, but exist on smaller wild grass seeds. But when the population expands and the birds take to raiding crops the damage is often devastating. The indigenous farming methods in which small boys were used to scare the birds away from the small fields were reasonably effective, but on the enlarged modernized farms, such methods are of no use. By flying aircraft over the flocks the birds can be kept on the move – but the cost is prohibitive – other methods tried include the use of sounds such as explosions or imitations of birds' calls, but these were of little or no use.

Most of the controlling effort is directed at the roosting sites or nesting colonies where they are attacked in some of the most blood-curdling ways man has devised for killing wild animals: the colonies are burnt with flame-throwers, destroyed with explosives, and sprayed from the air. The latter method is known to have killed some 400,000,000 queleas in a five-year period in South Africa alone and, while it is possible that these drastic measures may in some way control the quelea numbers in a limited area, it is fairly certain that they will not have any lasting effect on the total population. This is because the quelea

occurs over an enormous part of Africa, many areas of which are far from cultivation where the birds do no harm, and it is the overspill from the colonies of these areas which will replace the ones man exterminates.

Many other species of weaver are sociable to a greater or lesser degree, but the sociable weaver (*Philitairus socius*) is among the very few birds to co-operate in building a large single nest structure used by more than one pair. The nest may be up to 10 feet high and 25 feet long – the only other birds building a communal nest of comparable complexity being the quaker parakeets of South America (*Myiopsitta monachus*). Beneath a superstructure, which forms a waterproof thatched roof, the individual nest chambers are built with their entrance tunnels finishing flush with the bottom of the roof. The nests are used for year after year and the maintenance of the nest is performed by all the members of the colony. As time goes on other species of animal take advantage of the shelter and move in, and so gradually the nest houses a complete community.

In general appearance the weavers are a variable family; many species are rather dull sparrow-like birds while some species, such as the whydahs, have long, wide tails. Yet others such as the fodies and the bishops are quite brilliantly

Orange-breasted waxbill with its carefully-woven nest. Waxbills are occasionally known as weaver finches

(Below) swee waxbill, also shown with its carefully-woven nest

plumaged. The red bishop (*Euplectes orix*) and the closely related Zanzibar red bishop (*E. nigroventris*) are among the most brilliantly plumaged; the males are bright scarlet above with varying amounts of velvety-black on the face and upper parts. The smallest member of the genus *Euplectes* is the golden bishop (*E. afer*) which is similar to the red bishop, but it is only four and a half inches long and has the red plumage replaced by golden-yellow.

Although the starlings (Sturnidae) have a wide distribution, and a considerable number of 110 or so species are confined to Asia or the western Pacific, several genera are predominantly African in their distribution. Like the familiar European starling (Sturnus vulgaris), one of the characteristic features of many of these starlings is their glossy iridescent plumage, which many species possess. The starlings of the genus *Lamprotornis* are among the 'glossiest' of the starlings; their plumages being shimmering iridescent blues, greens or violets, which glitter in the bright African sun. One of the most familiar species is the blue-eared glossy starling (*Lamprotornis chalybaeus*) which is common in the East African game parks. It is normally a metallic green bird, but as the light moves so it may appear bluish or even golden-bronze. Even more stunning than the glossy starling, is the violet or amethyst starling (*Cinnyricinclus leucogaster*), which is widespread in Africa south of the Sahara. It is one of the smallest species of starling, being not much more than six inches long; the male is whitish below and a metallic violet above which, depending on the light conditions, may appear bluish or purplish-crimson. The females and young are quite drab in contrast.

The six spreo or superb starlings (*Spreo* species) all have fairly restricted distributions within Africa, but where they occur they are often abundant and obvious birds. They are noisy and the superb starling (*Spreo superbus*), which is more common in East African parks, provides one of the characteristic sounds of the African dawn in the bush – it utters a wide range of twitterings, warblings, chatterings, and whistles, including mimicry of other birds, as do many species of starling.

The oxpeckers are considered to be closely related to the starlings, although they exhibit several structural differences. There are only two species; the red-billed oxpecker (*Buphagus erythrorhynchus*), which is found on the eastern side of Africa, and the yellow-billed oxpecker (*B. africanus*), which is found on the western side. Apart from the difference implied in their name, the two species are very similar. They are entirely

Malachite sunbird,
feeding on an erica
(see orange-breasted
sunbird on page 75)

(Right) yellow-backed
sunbird, one of several
species with brilliant
scarlet breasts

70

*Burchell's glossy
starling with plumage
glinting in the sunlight*

73

(Left) superb starling.
This and Burchell's
glossy starling (see
previous page) are two
of a group of birds often
extremely tame

(Right) orange-breasted
sunbird, feeding.
Similar in habits to the
humming-birds of the
New World, sunbirds
feed on nectar and
insects (see also
pages 70 and 71)

dependent on the occurrence of large mammals for their food supply as they both feed almost entirely on ticks and a few species of flies, mainly parasitic. They are adapted to their mode of life by having a stiffened, almost woodpecker-like tail to support them as they clamber around, short toes with extremely sharp claws, and short, powerful, decurved bills. They carry out their searches on a wide variety of mammals ranging from wart hogs to giraffes; the most popular 'dining tables' are buffalo, rhinoceros and eland. The only times these animals ever seem to show any signs of annoyance is when the oxpecker gets too close to the eyes or ears, otherwise the oxpecker is left to make a thorough search of the whole body.

The family Nectariniidae (sunbirds), is yet another characteristic of the Old World tropics, being in many ways an ecological replacement of the humming-birds which are confined to the New World. The sunbirds are by no means confined to Africa – some species occurring through India and South-East Asia – but it is in Africa that the greatest variety and most beautiful species are to be found. One of the most wide-spread species is the scarlet-chested sunbird (*Nectarinia hunteri*), found over most of Africa south of the Sahara except in the densely forested areas and the really arid regions. It is often seen in gardens and is usually one of the first birds to be noticed by visitors to this region. It is basically black, with an iridescent green forehead and chin, and brilliant scarlet chest with metallic blue tips to some of the feathers.

Although sunbirds can be described as the Old World equivalents of the humming-birds they differ in many ways. Like the humming-birds they are small, often brilliantly coloured, often

Black-headed herons in flight

iridescent. However, they cannot hover, and since they are nectar-feeders like the humming-birds they often get at nectar by piercing the base of the bloom. To help them in their feeding, the bill of nearly all species of sunbird is fairly long, curved and pointed; the tongue is hollow, long and can be protruded for some distance. Another species of sunbird common over much of southern Africa is the malachite sunbird (*Nectarinia famosa*); the female, as in most species, is rather drab, but the male is a beautiful metallic green, with a long tail and long decurved bill. The golden-winged sunbird (*N. reichenowi*), on the other hand, has a very restricted distribution, being confined to highland areas of Uganda, Kenya, northern Tanzania, and the eastern Congo at altitudes of between about 5,000 and 11,000 feet. Within its limited range it is often quite abundant – and is certainly one of the most striking-looking

of sunbirds with its sickle-shaped decurved bill The golden colouring of the wings and tail i found in the plumage of both sexes – so thi female is not so drab. In full breeding plumage th male is a very impressive bird; apart from hi golden wings and tail he moults into deep reddish brown plumage with a coppery, golden sheen and has long central tail-streamers.

To the east of Africa, separated by a gap o nearly 250 miles lies the 240,000 square-mile island of Madagascar. This island, regarded as a subregion of the Ethiopian region by zoo geographers, is of considerable interest to naturalists. As in Australia, in its isolation many interesting and unique animals have evolved. In fact, Madagascar has one of the most distinctive faunas in the whole world; unfortunately it is also one of the least studied. It was on this island that the bird which is thought to have given rise to

(Below) herons stalk their prey by stealth; here a green-backed heron has caught a fish

Palm weaver building its
nest. This is one of the
simplest nests built by
weavers—the most
complex being that of
the sociable weaver

the tales of the legendary *roc* lived. *Aepyornis* was a giant flightless bird and even if the Arab traders of the late Middle Ages did not actually see the living birds they would have seen the enormous eggs which can still, to this day, be found on the Madagascan plains.

The birds endemic to Madagascar include mesites, vanga-shrikes, ground-rollers, couas, asities and cuckoo-rollers. The ground-rollers (Brachypteraciidae) are a group of five species which, while clearly related to rollers from other parts of the world, show several fundamental differences, the most obvious of which is that they are long-legged birds adapted for a terrestrial existence. In appearance they differ quite widely from each other, but unfortunately very little is known about their habits. Similarly the cuckoo-roller (*Leptosomus discolor*) shows some similarity to the true rollers (*Coraciidae*), but is also

placed in a separate family (Leptosomatidae).

The 13 species of vanga-shrikes (Vangidae) are an amazingly diverse family, of considerable interest to ornithologists. Their diversity is perhaps most apparent in the structure of the bill which ranges from the shrike-like (*Leptopterus madagascarinus*) to the sickle-bill (*Falculea palliata*) and the enormous bill of the helmet bird (*Euryceros prevostii*). Unfortunately yet again there is little information on the birds in the wild and it is not known precisely how these different bills are used.

The two species of asity (*Philepitta* species) and the two species of false sunbird (*Neodrepanis* species) are grouped together to form the family Phileptidae, which is endemic to Madagascar. The false sunbirds, as their name implies, seem to be an ecological replacement of the sunbirds, while the asities are a pitta-type bird.

(Below) portrait of
Ross's turaco, or
plantain-eater; in
flight the bird shows
deep purplish-red wings

Immature white-winged
black terns roosting on
Lake Nakuru; although
this species does breed
in Africa, the vast
majority of them are
Palearctic migrants

THE NEOTROPICAL REGION

From the deserts of New Mexico to the rain forests
and High Andes of South America

The Neotropical region – Central and South America – is a rich and varied one. Over 2,500 bird species – well over a quarter of the world's total – are found here. One of the reasons for such a wide variety is the extensive range of habitats which occur. Although the Ethiopian region (Africa) has an area of nearly 11,500,000 square miles, compared with just over 7,000,000 for the Neotropical region, the Neotropical region stretches from 24°N. to 55°S. – Africa has a range 12° less. South America also has twice as much of its land area above 5,000 feet, and over three times as much rain forest. This latter is probably the most important single factor governing the number of species found on the continental mass; rain forest is the richest, most diverse and relatively stable habitat in which a large number of species can co-exist.

The Neotropical region has many characteristic families: the ovenbirds (Furnariidae), toucans (Ramphastidae), tanagers (Thraupidae), cotingas (Cotingidae), antbirds (Formicariidae), puffbirds (Bucconidae), motmots (Momotidae), humming-birds (Trochilidae), rheas (Rheidae), tinamous (Tinamidae) are all families which are almost exclusively South American. Many other families are well represented, such as trogons, tyrant flycatchers and parrots.

The humming-birds have long attracted man's attention – like the beautiful birds of paradise of New Guinea they were once sought after for their dazzling plumage to satisfy the whims of the millinery trade. Very often the whole bird and even clusters of birds were used to decorate the hats of fashionable ladies. Fortunately this has now ceased, and they are only exported live for the pet trade. Although this trade does not involve the vast numbers of the skin trade, hundreds must die each year in order that a few shivering specimens reach the pet shops of Europe and North America.

These birds are often described as 'living jewels' – and they certainly live up to that name. There are over 300 species – mostly only a couple of inches long and nearly all confined to Central and South America, though a few species reach North America. One species, the ruby-throated humming-bird (*Archilochus colubris*) breeds as far north as eastern Canada.

Humming-birds are the only birds which can really fly backwards: they hover in front of orchids and other flowers of the forest, feeding on nectar and insects, then when they have finished they back away before darting off in search of more food. In order to perform these miraculous feats of flight, the humming-bird's wing is beating at speeds of anything between 30 and 50 times each second. Or rather the wing is almost revolving, because this is the real secret of the humming-bird's extraordinary manoeuvrability; as the wings beat they are rotated in a figure-of-eight shape and, by altering the angle of the wings the 'hummer' can perform these seemingly impossible feats of aviation.

The beauty of the humming-birds comes not so much from elaborate trailing plumes – though some species do have them – but mainly from the iridescence of their plumage. With every movement the bird makes, the feathers shimmer and glitter; greens, blues, golds, reds, violets, purples, glowing as if lit from within the bird. Every time the bird moves the colours change as the angle of the light on the iridescent feathers varies. The colours are almost impossible to capture with a camera – and even more impossible in words.

The humming-birds also show quite remarkable variation in their morphology. The smallest known bird in the world is the tiny bee humming-bird (*Mellisuga helenae*) which is found only on Cuba and Ile des Pines. It is less than two and a half inches long and weighs less than two grams – considerably less than many beetles! The largest species is the giant humming-bird of the Andes. It grows to a length of eight and a half inches – about the same size as a starling – but apart from its large size it is one of the least spectacular species of humming-bird. A species which closely approaches the same overall length as the giant humming-bird is the sword-billed humming-bird – the bill is nearly half the bird's

Luxuriant mountain woodland with bananas and coffee, on the island of Trinidad

total length. Several species, such as the streamer-tail (*Trochilus polytmus*), the marvellous spatule-tail (*Loddigesia mirabilis*), and the crimson topaz (*Topaza pella*) have long tail plumes, or streamers.

There are several other interesting features relating to humming-birds – not least is their ability to go into a state of torpor. Being such small birds and having a high metabolic rate means that at night, or during inclement weather, they could be in danger of using up all their energy in merely maintaining their body temperature. In order to overcome this problem some species are able to lower their body temperature and go into a state of torpor – somewhat similar to the state in which bats spend the winter or day-time – and thereby conserve valuable energy resources. The torpid birds fluff out their feathers to provide insulation, the heartbeat and rate of breathing slows down, the

body temperature drops, and they become more or less oblivious to their surroundings. They also have a way of locking their feet onto their perch, as most roosting birds do, in order to prevent themselves falling off while they are asleep.

Trogons are among the world's most beautiful birds and many of the species found in Central and South America are superficially similar to others found in Africa and Asia. One group, however, is spectacularly different from most other trogons – the quetzals (*Pharomachrus*). Three of the species are only found in South America – but it is the fourth, from the highlands of Central America which is the most famous. This is the resplendent quetzal (*P. mocinno*), found mainly in the cloud forest zone. It is a brilliant iridescent green bird with the tail coverts extended to about two feet or more, and also some of the wing coverts extended to overlap onto the bird's flanks. Not surprisingly this stunning bird has long attracted man's attentions; it is the national bird of Guatemala, one of the countries in which it is found – in fact Guatemala's second largest city is Quezaltenango and the units of Guatemalan currency are *quetzales*. This respect for the quetzal in Central America is nothing new – when the Spanish *conquistadores* visited the Aztec capital of Tenochtitlan they found the rulers and dignitaries wearing elaborate head-dresses made from the feathers of the quetzal. Bernal Díaz, who chronicled the conquest of New Spain, as Mexico was then known, described how the great Montezuma when he came to meet Cortés was shaded by a canopy of quetzal feathers. Bernal Díaz also described how in Aztec zoos quetzals and many other birds were kept in aviaries and bred.

The Aztecs only plucked the plumes annually – showing much more foresight in conserving natural resources than 20th century man. One of the original head-dresses given by the Aztecs to their Spanish visitors is still preserved, and can be seen in the *Museum für Völkerkunde* in Vienna.

In many species of bird in which the male has elaborately developed plumes, he has little or nothing to do with the process of incubation and rearing of the young, but not so the quetzal. The quetzal's tail poses something of a problem for the male, who nests in holes in rotting trees. What can he do with a tail over twice as long as his body? Apparently, after entering the nest he turns round so that he faces outwards, leaving his tail plumes doubled back over his head and projecting out of the entrance hole to wave in the breeze like the fronds of a fern.

Of all the South American birds few can be as well known or as popular as the toucans. The family Ramphastidae contains some 39 species known as toucans, aracaris, and toucanets, more or less according to size. Most species are colourful, but, in fact, the best known species, the toco toucan (*Ramphastos toco*) is one of the most soberly-plumaged. In its sombre black plumage with a white bib it looks as if it is wearing a tuxedo. It does, however, have one of the most spectacular bills in a family renowned for impressive bills. Among the most colourful members of the family are the 11 species of aracaris (*Pteroglossus* species). They are often very sociable and wander through the forest in parties that may include more than one species - or even some of the larger toucans.

Although they feed mainly on fruits, toucans and their relatives will also pillage the nests of a variety of birds and eat any eggs or nestlings they

Blue-crowned motmot, in which the tail has lost the barbs along part of its length, giving a 'racquet-tailed' effect

find. Although the plumage of these and many other tropical birds appears gaudy and you would expect it to stand out – making the bird very conspicuous – some ornithologists have commented that providing the birds are at rest the seemingly bright plumage blends in with all the other splashes of light and colour among the foliage and blossoms of the forest.

The enormous bill of the toucan is not at all heavy – it is in fact more or less hollow – the interior consisting of a network of cellular structures filled with air. The actual purpose of the bill is still being argued about by ornithologists. One of the two main schools of thought suggests that it is a purely functional bill for gathering fruit and can also be used to reach otherwise inaccessible fruits; the other school believes that it has behavioural significance and that it may be used in displays such as courtship. It could, of course, combine both functions. These

and many other questions are at present unanswered for as yet very few South American birds have been studied in detail in the field.

The family Ramphastidae is part of the order Piciformes, which also includes the woodpeckers (Picidae), barbets (Capitonidae), jacamars (Galbulidae), honey-guides (Indicatoridae) and puffbirds and nunbirds (Bucconidae). Of these only the honey-guides are completely absent from South America. The jacamars, puffbirds and nunbirds are confined to South America. The woodpeckers are a colourful cosmopolitan family, and are widely distributed in South America – the piculets being particularly well represented with about 30 species occurring.

The 15 species of jacamar parallel very closely the bee-eaters of the Old World (Meropidae) in size, shape, plumage features, feeding and nesting habits, and yet they are quite unrelated. Typical of the family is the rufous-tailed jacamar (*Galbula*

(Below) rufous-tailed jacamar. The jacamars are similar in appearance (though completely unrelated) to the bee-eaters of the Old World
(Below right) of all the beautiful birds in Central and South America, the quetzal has probably fired man's imagination more than any other species

(Right) scarlet ibis are a difficult species to photograph as they tend to disperse away from the nesting colony for most of the day, large groups usually only being encountered as the light is failing

(Left) group of brown pelicans, which are confined to the New World and nearby Pacific islands. Here they are driving fish which they will scoop up in their capacious throat pouches. They are sociable birds

ruficauda) – it is about ten and a half inches long with iridescent metallic green upper parts; the throat is white, followed by a green breast band, and the rest of the under parts are a rich buffy-orange; it has a long slender bill. Like many species of jacamar it usually prefers fairly well-wooded areas – though it is always found around clearings rather than actually in woodlands. Like all other jacamars the rufous-tailed species is an insect-eater, capturing mainly Hymenoptera (bees, ants, wasps, etc.) on the wing as do the bee-eaters. The jacamar waits on a favourite perch and then makes short sallies at passing insects, returning in an arc to its perch after it has snapped up its prey.

The family Bucconidae – puffbirds, nunbirds, softwings and their relatives, is endemic to Central and South America and seems to have no ecological equivalent in the Old World, except possibly the terrestrial kingfisher. They are rather dumpy birds with fairly massive bills; they often feed by waiting on a prominent perch and darting out at passing insects of almost any type.

The barbets (Capitonidae) are a family more characteristic of the Old World than South America; although a dozen species are found, nearly all in the tropical rain forest. They are rather

passerine-like in general appearance, but have the massive bills characteristic of so many of the Piciformes, and zygodactylous feet.

One of the most fascinating of the birds endemic to the Neotropical region is the oilbird (*Steatornis caripensis*). It has no obvious close relatives and is placed in a family of its own – Steatornithidae. It is not particularly spectacular to look at, being rather like a large night-jar with a hawkish bill, and is found from Trinidad south to Venezuela, Colombia, Ecuador and Peru. It breeds in caves and it is from this habit that it has developed the remarkable ability to use echo-location in order to navigate. The birds emit clicks, and by listening for the echoes are able to fly in the dark – an ability possessed by only one other group of birds, the swiftlets (*Collocalia*) of the Indian Ocean and South-East Asia. The oilbirds take their name from the fact that the young birds become extremely fat and at one time were collected and boiled to produce oil.

The family Todidae is a small group of five very closely related birds confined to the Caribbean area. They are all about the size of wrens, with bright green plumage above and red and white below. The motmots (Momotidae) are another family confined to the New World, particularly Central America. There are only eight species in the family, all of which are handsome birds – the blue-crowned motmot being perhaps the most beautiful. Apart from being beautifully-plumaged it has a 'racquet' tail, which is formed by the barbs on the two long central tail feathers breaking away to leave a disc at the end of each feather. When the bird is excited the racquets are bobbed from side to side like a pendulum.

Several passerine families are confined to the New World – many of them are rather insignificant 'little brown birds' which present considerable identification problems to the visiting bird-watcher. The family Dendrocolaptidae comprises about 50 species known as woodcreepers – all of which are brown warbler-like birds, as are many of the 200 or so Furnariidae (ovenbirds, thornbirds, earthcreepers, spinetails and so forth). The family Formicariidae (antbirds) includes a number of dull brown birds, but some others are considerably more colourful than the previous two families. Other passerine families more or less endemic to the Neotropical region include Oxyruncidae, which contains a single species

Like its Asiatic counterpart, the Carolina or wood duck is very colourful, and yet it is mainly found in temperate regions and does not extend into truly tropical habitats. The duck family is one of the few large groups of birds where really colourful species are found outside the tropics

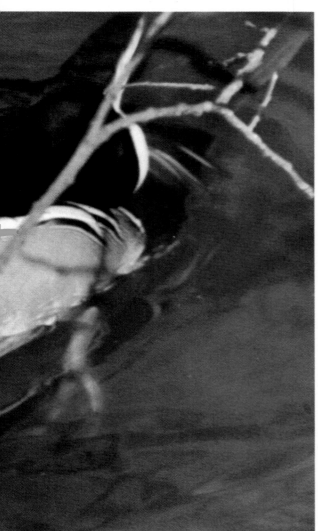

The magpie-jay is found in arid scrub-forest in Central America. The tail is so long that when the bird is in flight it streams behind with a wave-like motion

known as the sharpbill, and the Phytotomidae, the three species of plant-cutter.

One of the most diverse families of the Neotropical rain forest is the Cotingidae. Comprising nearly 100 species they range in size from sparrow-sized birds to some nearly as big as a crow; most species have strange displays and startling calls, and some have bizarre feather ornamentation. Perhaps the most dazzling of the cotingas are the five species belonging to the genus *Cotinga*. They are all rather dumpy birds about seven to nine inches long, the males having brilliant, almost garish plumage which is even brighter than that of kingfishers – bright turquoise contrasting with bands of black, deep purple, or plum colour depending on the species. In contrast to the glittering plumage of the *Cotinga* species, the ornate umbrella bird (*Cephalopterus ornatus*), which is the largest species in the family, is a rather plainly-coloured bird. However, whatever it may lack in colour it makes up for in ornamentation. Its most striking feature is its crest which rises steeply from the forehead for about two and a half inches as stiff quills which then become filamentous, forming a mop of feathers. As its name implies, these feathers form an 'umbrella' over the bird's head. The ornate umbrella bird also has a long pendulous wattle some two inches long at the base of the neck which is covered in feathers.

The four species of bellbirds (*Procnias* species) are so named because their voices sound just

Male Guianan cock-of-the-rock. This brilliantly coloured bird also performs a remarkable display, in which several males gather together to 'dance' in a forest

like a bell striking – the sound will carry across valleys in the forests for around three-quarters of a mile. But of all the beautiful and interesting birds of the family Cotingidae, it is the two species of cock-of-the-rock which are the most famous. They are among the most spectacular of all the birds in the world, combining colourful plumage with fascinating displays. The two species are very similar, differing mainly in intensity of colour. The Guianan, or golden, cock-of-the-rock (*Rupicola rupicola*) is found in the Guianas and between the Orinoco and Amazon Rivers; the Andean cock-of-the-rock (*R. peruviana*) is found along the Andes from Colombia to Bolivia. Both species are mainly found in tropical and subtropical forest in montane regions, their ranges being separated by the lowlands. They are about 13 inches long with a rather short, stout build; the bill and feet are stout and strong. The females are rather dull, but the males are brilliant: the Andean cock-of-the-rock has scarlet head and body, jet-black tail and primaries, and grey inner wing feathers; the male Guianan cock-of-the-rock is bright golden-

orange with blackish-brown wings and tail. Apart from its colour the crests are the other most noticeable features of the cock-of-the-rock. Both species have crests which start between the bill and eye, and sweep up in a laterally-flattened double fan going back over the head. In the Guianan species the crest has a dark subterminal band. Even in a zoo, male cock-of-the-rocks are an impressive sight, but they only really achieve their true glory on their display grounds deep in the tropical forest. In the display of the Guianan cock-of-the-rock (the Andean species is probably very similar, but has been little studied) the males gather at clearings in the forest where a break in the canopy allows light to reach the forest floor. Each male has his own particular perch and moves between his perch and the ground below; every time he lands his wings sweep the ground, gradually clearing a bare patch. As he flies to and fro the wings produce a whistling noise – the end of the web on the outer primary feather on each wing is reduced to a thin tip, and it is this feather which produces the sound. As the bird flies down, a white wing-bar – concealed when the

The burrowing owl is widely distributed in the more open and arid areas of Central and South-America, where it nests in burrows in the open ground

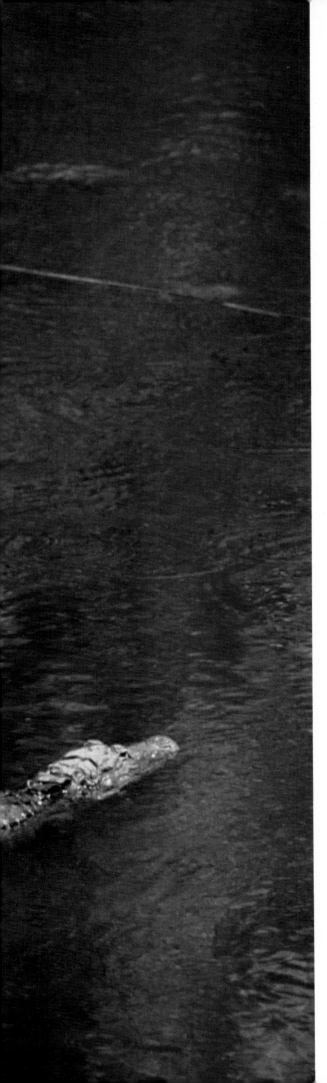

bird is perching – also becomes apparent. Once on the ground, the cock-of-the-rock performs a complex series of bows, at the same time making squawks and ringing notes; the head is also held horizontally and the crests spread in such a way as almost completely to cover the head.

Like the Cotingidae, members of the family Pipridae – manakins – perform elaborate, often communal, displays. It has been postulated that elaborate displays have evolved in tropical fruit- and nectar-feeding birds because there is such an abundance of food that the males do not need to take any part in the rearing of the young. Typical of the family are Gould's manakin (*Manacus vitellinus*) and the black and white manakin (*M. manacus*). In this genus the displays are highly developed; a number of males gather and compete for females on a communal display ground – which is usually an area with plenty of young saplings close together. The sight of as many as 70 males gathered together all performing their elaborate posturing, whirring their wings and emitting a wide variety of calls, squeaks and grunts, is impressive to say the very least. But the species which has been studied in the greatest detail is probably the yellow-thighed manakin (*Pipra mentalis*), which occurs in Central and northern South America. The male is mainly jet-black with a brilliant red cap and yellowish throat, sulphur-yellow thighs and sulphur-yellow under the wings; the female is a dull olive-green.

At the beginning of the breeding season the male selects a display perch which is preferably a straight, horizontal branch free from twigs and without any creepers growing along it for several feet. Up to about five males will gather in a fairly small area – their perches usually being some 20–45 feet high. As soon as a female appears in the vicinity of the display perches the males are roused into action, accompanying the display with a variety of noises. These noises are partly vocal, but some are mechanically produced by the modified wing feathers. The main forms of the display (many other manakins probably have similar ones) are described as 'about facing', 'circling flight', and 'backward sliding'; darting to and fro is carried on between the main displays.

One of the strangest groups of birds endemic to South America is the family Anhimidae – the screamers. Only three species are known and they are real oddities of the bird world. Thought to be distantly related to waterfowl and also flamingoes, all three species are nearly three feet long and vaguely like a game-bird such as a turkey in general appearance, with stubby de-curved bill, powerful legs, with only a slight trace of webbing between the toes, and long, sharp

Great blue heron, in the subtropical Florida Everglades, pauses as an alligator slides past

99

Red fan parrot, one of the most spectacular of the parrots found in the rain forest; when alarmed it raises the feathers at the back of its head

spurs on the wings. Other anatomical peculiarities include a very thick skin which has a complicated layer of air sacs beneath it and unusually pneumatic bones – all birds have air spaces in many of the bones, but in the screamer even the smaller bones of the wings and feet are hollow. The feathers which cover the body grow evenly all over, not in regular patterns as in most other birds; the only other birds which have this peculiarity are ostriches, penguins and colies. As they take flight the screamers' wings make a loud swishing noise, but it is their harsh trumpet-like calls which have given them their name. The famous English writer and ornithologist, W. H. Hudson, who spent his early years in South America, described the voice of the crested screamer (*Chauna torquata*) thus: 'The voice is very powerful. . . . it is exercised in a kind of singing performance in which the male and female join, and which produces the effect of harmony. The male begins, the female takes up her part, and then with marvellous strength and spirit they pour forth a torrent of strangely-contrasted sounds – some bassoon-like in their depth and volume, some like drum-beats and others long, clear and ringing. It is the loudest animal-sound of the pampas, and its jubilant, martial character strongly affects the mind in all

that silent, melancholy wilderness.' Other writers were not quite as enthusiastic about the vocal talents as Hudson – the sound is more often referred to as a deafening din!

The three species of flamingo (Phoenicopteridae) occurring in South America are not all birds of the warmer coastal and inland waters. The greater flamingo (*Phoenicopterus ruber ruber*) closely related to other populations in Europe, Asia and Africa is found in the Caribbean and northern South America and another population (*P. r. chilensis*), sometimes regarded as a separate

Blue and yellow macaw, preening. The macaws are the largest members of the parrot family and are found in Central and South America. The massive bill is powerful enough to crack Brazil nuts

(Left) mealy parrot, one of the group of predominantly greenish parrots known collectively as 'Amazon parrots'

(Right) silver-throated tanager. Tanagers are among the most colourful birds of the South American tropics

species, occurs in southern South America. The most interesting of the South American flamingo colonies are those in Bolivia which were only discovered as recently as 1957. At altitudes around 14,000 feet above sea level the Chilean flamingo breeds together with James's flamingo (*Phoenicoparrus jamesi*) and the Andean flamingo (*P. andinus*). In contrast to the lush tropical rain forest found at lower altitudes, the habitat found around the high altitude Andean lakes is barren and desolate in extreme. The lakes are often devoid of almost all life except minute forms of aquatic life and the flamingoes which feed on them. Like the lesser flamingoes of the East African soda lakes which feed upon the blue-green algae, the flamingoes of the High Andes are adapted to feeding on algae – in their case the algae is reddish or orange; the Andean lakes are also highly mineralized.

The discovery of James's flamingo in 1957 was particularly important as until then the bird was virtually unknown; it had been recognized as a separate species in the late 19th century from skins sent back from Chile by an English business-man in the 1850s, and from then on remained virtually unknown until the discovery of their breeding colony in 1957. If the habitat of these high altitude lakes is desolate, then the weather is even worse; even in summer, storms of rain, hail, sleet or snow are of common occurrence, and in winter the water becomes cold enough to freeze – although it may be many times saltier than sea water. Fortunately for the flamingoes many of the lakes are fed by streams of warm or even hot water, the area in which they occur having a lot of volcanic activity.

Second only to the humming-birds in their beauty are the tanagers (Thraupinae) which, like the former, are more or less confined to South America. The largest groups of tanagers are the 46 species comprising the genus *Tangara* and the 22 species in the genus *Tanagra*. The

(Left) flame-crowned tanager

(Right) a few species extend into the temperate regions, such as the scarlet or Brazilian tanager, which is found as far north as Canada, but the greatest variety is to be found in the rain forest

Tangara tanagers, with the exception of three Central American species, all occur in South America. They are medium-sized finch-like birds often with brilliantly coloured plumage. They nearly all occur in the forests, usually living in the canopy. They are sociable and often move through the tree-tops in parties mixed with other species of bird. Because of their colourful plumage many species are kept in cages all over the world – the most popular being species such as the seven-coloured tanager (*Tangara fastuosa*) which occurs in eastern Brazil, and the blue-necked tanager (*T. cyanocollis*) which is widespread over much of northern South America.

Although the brilliant plumages look distinctive enough in a photograph, or a caged specimen, identifying these birds in the field is another matter entirely. Flitting around high in the forest canopy among the sunlight, leaves and blossoms, their colours are barely visible; they also move around in a relatively silent manner – not giving any helpful calls by which they could be recognized. They are also very active little birds and are constantly on the move.

Emerald-spotted tanager

Mrs. Wilson's tanager

107

(*Left*) *close-up of a magpie tanager—the bird takes its name from its long, magpie-like tail*

The species of the genus *Tanagra* are known as euphonias and unlike the previous group are fairly noisy, uttering a clear, whistling song. They are a close-knit group of stubby-billed, dumpy, short-tailed birds, mainly blue, yellow and red. They are almost exclusively berry-eaters, some species feeding virtually entirely on the berries of mistletoes. The euphonias are thought to be fairly closely related to the chlorophonias, (*Chlorophonia* species), but unlike the chlorophonias they lack any green in the plumage.

One of the best known species of tanager is the scarlet tanager (*Piranga olivacea*), in which the male is brilliant scarlet with jet-black wings – the reason this species is better known than most is that it is one of the half-dozen or so species of tanager to be found in North America.

Although most tanagers are finch-like there are several groups which show marked differences, as their names imply. The shrike tanagers (*Lanio* species) have the same sort of proportions as the shrikes – with a fairly long tail and a slightly hooked bill. They feed on insects which they hunt for in the forest canopy. The single species in the genus *Rhodinocicla*, the rose-breasted thrush tanager, (*R. rosea*), shows a striking resemblance to a thrush in its general shape and build, though in colour it is more spectacular than most thrushes – the male is a rosy magenta on the underside and forehead, while the female is a bright orange. The magpie tanager (*Cissopsis leveriana*) is only five or six inches long, but the tail adds a similar length; this, together with its distinctive black and white plumage, gives rise to its popular name. Closely related to the tanagers is the swallow tanager (*Tersina viridis*) which is usually placed in a separate subfamily of its own, the Tersininae. Although it shows many superficial similarities to the tanagers it has many important differences, particularly in its anatomy.

(*Right*) *the seven-coloured tanager (see pages 103–107 for other species of tanager)*

THE TROPICAL OCEANS AND ISLANDS

Tropical islands have always held some sort of fascination for the city-dweller – obviously escapism is at the back of man's day-dreams of the idyllic life in the South Seas; ornithologists are no exception. Those ornithologists fortunate enough to visit the few remaining unspoilt oceanic islands have put up very strong cases for their conservation – islands such as the Seychelles and Aldabra in the Indian Ocean and the Galapagos in the Pacific. Already several of the islands in the Seychelles group have been overrun by 'civilization' – tourist brochures offer package-holidays and estate agents offer building plots on land that once belonged to the plants and the birds. Aldabra is more fortunate – a projected air base has been abandoned and visitors to the island are mainly confined to research scientists. What then are the birds which are so fascinating on tropical islands?

The birds found on oceanic islands can be broadly separated into three groups: breeding seabirds, resident landbirds, and resting migrants or winter visitors. It is the first two groups which are of particular interest.

Perhaps the most characteristic seabirds of the tropical islands are the tropic birds (Phaethontidae), frigate birds (Fregatidae) and skimmers (Rhynchopidae) all of which are 'endemic' to tropical seas; the terns are essentially tropical – three-quarters of the species breed in the tropics and the others occur on migration or spend the whole winter in tropical waters. By way of contrast only about one-quarter of the species of gull breeds in the tropics. Of the seabirds, the albatross (Diomedeidae) is one of the most famous – though few people who have not travelled will have actually seen one. It is the wandering albatross of the southern Atlantic and Antarctic which lays claim to having the greatest wing span of living birds, some 11–12 feet. All albatrosses have very long, narrow wings which enable them to utilize the slightest air current to their fullest advantage; however, once becalmed on the water or land (when the wind drops completely) they find it extremely difficult, if not impossible, to take off. Their long wings, though so superbly designed for gliding, are not much use for flapping flight.

Albatrosses, particularly the young birds, are known to sailors by a variety of rather derogatory names such as mollymawk or goney. Mollymawk is a corruption of two Dutch words, *mal* meaning foolish and *mok* meaning gull; the connection of goney with more modern equivalents such as goon is apparent – the birds presumably received these names from the way they sat and waited to be killed by the meat-hungry sailors visiting the islands. The name albatross is not derived, as most people think, from the latin *alba* meaning white, but is a corruption of the Spanish word *alcatraz* meaning pelican.

The boobies (Sulidae) likewise acquired a reputation for foolishness and the name stuck. In general shape and structure the boobies are very similar to the gannets – but the gannets are found in temperate waters at both ends of the world and boobies are found only in the tropics. Their feet are one of the most striking features of the boobies – they are often brightly coloured – red, blue, yellow or orange. Unlike the gannets many of the boobies nest in trees.

The six species of frigate bird are all very similar to each other – but quite easily distinguished from all other sea-birds. With a wing span of up to eight feet and a long forked tail they are rather like some kind of giant swift; and like the swift they are masters of the air. They hardly ever come to land, and they never settle on water as their plumage quickly becomes waterlogged. They take their name – and the alternative of man o'war birds – from their piratical feeding habits. Like the skuas of the temperate and polar waters the frigate birds obtain most of their food by harrying other species until they disgorge their last meal, which the frigate bird then swoops upon and catches in mid air. They also catch flying fish as they skim across the surface of the water, and will also prey on the eggs and young of other birds. But the frigate bird's most impressive feature of all is the gular sac of the

Rain forest vegetation along the coast of Maui, Hawaii. Extensive destruction of the Hawaiian forests has led to the extinction of several of the endemic bird species

111

male. Normally it is just a small piece of bright red flabby skin under his chin but when the bird is displaying, it is pumped full of air until he almost disappears behind it. Frigate birds soon learn that there are often refuse and scraps of food around man's habitations and sometimes they become quite tame. In the Pacific, the Samoan Islanders have used the frigate birds as a sort of 'pigeon post'. First of all the birds were enticed onto perches around a feeding area and then they were captured and a message attached to the wing. The birds would visit many other islands in the course of their foraging and within a few days the message would have been sent around the group of islands.

Like many other birds on oceanic islands, the tropic birds, also known as bo'sun birds on account of the marlin-spike they carry in their tail, are remarkably tame when incubating their eggs. They will sit until actually lifted off the nest – islanders in the southern Pacific used to pluck the long red streamers of the red-tailed tropic birds while they were incubating – without killing them – and use the streamers for decoration. There are three species of tropic bird, the red-billed (*Phaethon aethereus*), red-tailed (*P. rubricauda*), and white-tailed (*P. lepturus*). They are about the size of a medium-sized gull, the white-tailed species being slightly smaller than the other two. They have brilliant white plumage with some black markings and two extremely long tail feathers which may project two feet or more from the centre of the wedge-shaped tail.

The skimmers superficially resemble the terns –

being rather long-winged seabirds with dark upper parts, but as soon as the bill is seen it is quite apparent that they are an entirely separate group. Many birds have the upper mandible overhanging the lower, but the skimmers have the lower mandible much longer than the upper – quite unlike any other species of bird. The bill is laterally compressed to the thickness of a pen-knife blade; the upper mandible can be moved on the skull through a distance of about 20°; the lower mandible is slightly flexible. The skimmers use this structure to obtain their food in a most unusual way – they fly close to the surface of the water and literally plough it with the bill, which enables them to scoop up plankton and other small forms of life.

There are three species of skimmer – the black skimmer (*Rhynchops nigra*) found on the lakes, rivers, and coasts of tropical America; the African skimmer (*R. flavirostris*) and the Indian skimmer (*R. albicollis*) both found in similar habitats to the American species. Another unique feature of the skimmers is the shape of the eye pupil – they are the only birds to have a vertical pupil. This is an adaptation for night vision; during the day the pupil is reduced to a narrow slit, protecting the sensitive retina, but at night the pupil opens and the birds can see even in very poor light – they will feed on the plankton which rises to the surface of the water during the night.

Many other sea-birds and also birds such as egrets and herons occur on oceanic islands but it is the land-birds which give each island group its particularly distinctive character.

(Above) noddy terns on an islet in the lagoon of the atoll of Aldabra

(Right) red-tailed tropic bird in flight. The long tail streamers give the bird its alternative name of bo'sun bird— named after its marlin spike-like tail

(Below) White-tailed tropic bird on its nest. These birds are usually so tame that they will not shift from their eggs until actually lifted

Of all the tropical oceanic islands probably the most famous are the Galapagos Islands which the young Charles Darwin visited when he travelled around the world on the *Beagle*. Here he saw some remarkable animals – giant tortoises, marine iguanas, flightless cormorants and some rather dull finch-like birds. Studying the collections and notes (made by himself, Captain Fitzroy and others on the islands) helped the young Darwin formulate some of his theories of evolution and natural selection. The flightless cormorant is typical of many birds found on oceanic islands which have their wings reduced, often to the extent of being utterly useless for flight. It has been suggested that, in the case of land-birds, flight on a tropical island would be a disadvantage, and that once a species has reached the island and colonized it, then natural selection will operate to reduce the flying abilities of the birds, as a bird flying on a small oceanic island stands a very good chance of being blown out to sea in a gale or storm.

The most notable group of flightless birds are the rails. These are all fairly small birds about the size of a bantam, all ground-dwellers, usually living and feeding in dense undergrowth, particularly marshy areas. They tend to avoid flight under normal conditions, and it is perhaps not surprising that a number of the island forms of rails are flightless – some, such as the rail found on the Indian Ocean island of Aldabra, are flightless but closely related to rails occurring elsewhere which can still fly. However, flightlessness does have one major disadvantage – it leaves the bird vulnerable to certain predators.

The arrival of man on the tropical islands, with his cats and dogs, pigs and goats and rats and mice, spelt doom for a great many species. The dodos of the Mascarene islands were large flightless birds (distant relatives of the pigeons) which man and his animals exterminated by the late 18th century. They have now become symbolic of extinct animals in the same way that the panda is often used to represent rare or endangered species. The list of birds which have become extinct on oceanic islands is long and depressing; the causes are various but in the vast majority of cases the main culprit is man – particularly 'civilized' man. Rails have been exterminated from Tahiti, Jamaica, Laysan, the Aucklands, Chathams, Carolines, and Tristan da Cunha. They are probably extinct on several other islands, and have been reduced to dangerously low populations on yet others – and these are only one group of birds; many others have also suffered.

But to return to the Galapagos Islands,

Male great frigate bird blowing out his spectacular gular pouch as part of his display. These birds, among the finest fliers in the bird world, take their name from their piratical feeding habits

Darwin's finches from the Galapagos Islands are so named because the famous English naturalist was the first to realize that they were all closely related and probably descended from a common ancestor. (Right) Darwin's medium ground finch; (far right) Darwin's large ground finch is shown here

another characteristic of islands and island groups is that their birds are often strikingly different from any others in the world; this can be explained by the fact that a bird colonizing an oceanic island probably needs to fit into a rather different niche in the ecosystem from that which it occupied on the mainland, and so by the processes of natural selection the species will evolve rapidly and speciation may even take place.

Should the original invader recolonize, the two groups may be sufficiently different as to act as separate species. This is shown particularly well by the group of finches known as Darwin's finches (Geospizinae). There are 14 species altogether which, with one exception, occur on the Galapagos Islands: the exception is the Cocos finch (*Pinaroloxias inornata*).

Darwin's own words, taken from his *Journals*

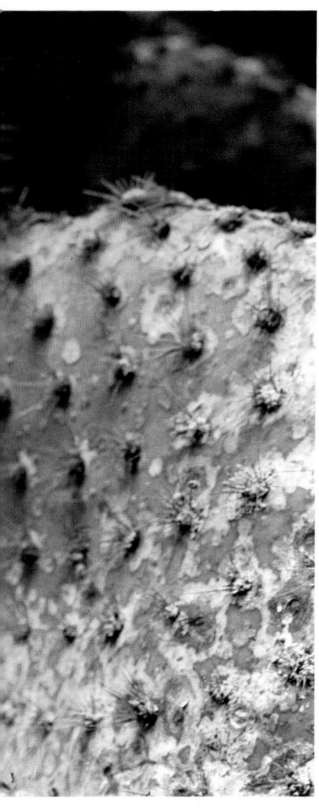

(1845), describe these fascinating birds as well as any subsequent writer's: 'The remaining land-birds form a most singular group of finches, related to each other in the structure of their beaks, short tails, form of body and plumage: there are thirteen species, which Mr Gould has divided into four sub-groups. . . . The males of all, or certainly of the greater number are jet-black; and the females (with perhaps one or two

(Left) the albatross is a characteristic seabird breeding on the islands of the southern oceans. Owing to their tameness they are easy prey for sailors who have given them nicknames such as mollymawk or goney. Grey-headed albatrosses are seen here courting

(Right and above) the flightless cormorant is confined to the Galapagos Islands and has completely lost the power of flight, as have so many other birds confined to oceanic islands. The cormorant above is drying its ineffectual wings amongst marine iguanas

119

Banded rail. This species is widespread and variable in appearance, occurring on many islands in the Australasian area and the western Pacific

exceptions) are brown. The most curious fact is the perfect gradation in the size of the beaks in the different species of *Geospiza*, from one as large as that of a hawfinch to that of a chaffinch, and . . . even to that of a warbler.'

The behaviour of some of the species has also attracted the attention of scientists – the woodpecker finch (*Camarhynchus pallidus*) is one of the few birds to use a tool. In the absence of a true woodpecker on the islands this particular finch has taken to feeding on grubs found in rotting trees and in cracks in the bark. If the bird is unable to reach the insect it is seeking, it may go and find a cactus spine on which to impale the insect in order to extract it. By no means all the woodpecker finches do it, as this behaviour is learnt and apparently passed on from individual to individual; some birds never learn the habit.

Another feature of the birds of oceanic islands is their tameness; as has already been mentioned many of the names of birds reflect their apparent stupidity and willingness to be captured – consequently sailors regarded them as 'goneys, boobies, mollymawks' and so forth. Darwin also noticed this and commented at some length: 'I will conclude my description of these islands, by giving an account of the extreme tameness of the birds . . . This disposition is common to all the terrestrial species; namely, to the mocking-thrushes, the finches, wrens, tyrant-flycatchers, the dove, and carrion-buzzard. All of them often approached sufficiently near to be killed with a switch and sometimes, as I myself tried, with a cap or hat. A gun here is almost superfluous; for with the muzzle I pushed a hawk off the branch of a tree . . . Formerly the birds appear to have been even tamer. Cowley (in the year 1684) says that the "Turtle-doves were so tame, that they

would often alight on our hats and arms . . ." At present, although certainly very tame, they do not alight on people's arms, nor do they suffer themselves to be killed in such large numbers. It is surprising that they have not become wilder; for these islands during the last 150 years have been frequently visited by bucaniers [*sic*] and whalers; and the sailors, wandering through the woods in search of tortoises, always take a cruel delight in knocking down the little birds.'

The trend of the birds to become shyer has continued; they are still remarkably tame – but no longer anything like as confiding as Cowley found them in 1684. The same applies to most other oceanic islands. Ever since Darwin's time scientists have realized that islands can be extremely useful laboratories for studying wild-life; recently several ornithologists have been studying exactly how birds colonize oceanic islands. The Tristan de Cunha group are a particularly good example (although they are outside the tropics) as they are over 2,000 miles from the nearest landfall in South America. During the early 1950s the islands were watched by ornithologists fairly continuously over a three-year period and during that time nine species of land-bird were recorded. A later expedition to Gough Island recorded six species during a three-week visit; and one species, the American purple gallinule is known to occur practically every year. None of these vagrants appears to be able to survive for more than a few days – presumably because it would be competing with species which are already well established – but this demonstrates that birds are able to travel vast distances, and to reach practically any island in the world.

Scientists investigating the factors controlling

the numbers of birds and the diversity of species occurring on islands have found that, although the situation is very complex, there is good evidence that the size of the island and its degree of isolation correlates with the number of species of birds occurring there. It has also been noted that, in general, a bird inhabiting an island will occupy a broader niche in the ecosystem and possibly exclude a greater variety of species than it would normally under mainland conditions.

Another group of islands which have only recently come into the public eye are the Seychelles and the atoll of Aldabra. The latter was saved from becoming an airbase and is now a research station for biologists. The former are being 'developed' as a tourist resort and recently an international airport was opened. One of the main advertised attractions of the islands is that they are a haven for wildlife – yet the very people who visit these islands on their package holidays and cruises are likely to be the destroyers of the island sanctuaries.

The Seychelles have already lost their parrot (*Psittacula eupatria wardi*) and their white-eye (*Zosterops semiflava*). Their owl (*Otus insularis*), thought to be extinct for nearly half a century, was rediscovered a few years ago; but how long it will survive against the spread of holiday bungalows for tourists is unknown. The fody is restricted to Cousin Island – fortunately now a bird sanctuary.

In the Indian Ocean the islands which can claim the most drastic reduction of their bird species at the hands of man are the Mascarenes. The Mascarene Islands (Réunion, Rodriguez, and Mauritius) were discovered in 1505 and at that time they were uninhabited. The first residents on the islands were probably the convicts

Apapane (right) and amakihi (below) from the Hawaiian island of Kauai. Birds such as these were once widespread and abundant, but many species are now extinct in the Hawaiian islands

Madagascar fody. These colourful birds have colonized the atoll of Aldabra, the Seychelles, Rodriguez and Mauritius—a different species being known from each area

introduced by the Dutch in 1598, but this was nearly a century before any really permanent settlements were established. However, the position of the islands must have been well known to sailors and many must have stopped to provision their ships with water, tortoises and birds. The islands were often compared with the 'Garden of Eden' – with their beautiful mountains, clear rivers and streams, lush forests and mild sub-tropical climate; on Réunion, the mountain peaks rise to over 10,000 feet. Many of the now extinct birds are known only from vague descriptions of early travellers but there is evidence that the islands were once inhabited by some 28 species of land-bird, all but one being found nowhere else in the world; at least 24 of these are now extinct – and the others are in a none too healthy state.

Most people have heard of the dodo from Mauritius (*Raphus cucullatus*) which became extinct towards the end of the 17th century – extirpated by the cats, rats, pigs and other animals brought by the English and French settlers; not so well known are the closely related solitaire (*Raphus solitarius*) which disappeared from Réunion by about 1750, and another solitaire (*Pezophaps solitaria*) which was found on Rodriguez and became extinct between 1750 and 1800. All that remains of these rather bizarre birds are bones and a few sketches, paintings and descriptions by early visitors to the islands. At one time there was a stuffed dodo in the Ashmolean Museum, Oxford; this specimen became somewhat moth-eaten and it was decided to destroy it – fortunately for posterity, an assistant pulled the head and a foot from the fire – these are

now unique specimens. Other birds once found on the Mascarene islands but now extinct include rails (*Aphanapteryx*), a large parrot on Mauritius, (*Lophopsittacus mauritianus*) and parrots on the other two islands (*Necropsittacus rodericanus* and *Mascarinus mascarinus*); owls were also known from the islands and some 23 skins of the crested starling (*Fregilupus varius*) are all that remains of a bird once widespread.

If the story of the effect of man on the bird-life of the Mascarene Islands seems depressing then the story of the Hawaiian Islands is that of an all-time 'eco-disaster'. Of some 68 species of land-bird once found on the Hawaiian islands some 40 are now extinct. Of these the most interesting were the endemic honeycreepers (Drepanidae). Like Darwin's finches, the honeycreepers had radiated to fill most of the niches in the ecosystem of the Hawaiian islands, but unlike Darwin's rather dull looking Galapagos finches, the honeycreepers were often extremely attractive and colourful. Very little is known about the precise cause for their wholesale extinction, but in many cases the destruction of the forests which originally covered the islands must be an important factor.

Another factor which has probably played a part in the decline of many of the more recently extinct birds is the introduction of alien species. Like New Zealand, settlers in Hawaii have released countless species of birds from all over the world – the introduced land-birds now outnumber the native species. For many of the species still hovering on the brink of extinction the prospects are pretty gloomy but for one there is a ray of hope – it is the Hawaiian goose or néné (*Branta sandvicensis*). These birds once numbered an estimated 25,000 but by the 1950s only about 35 remained alive in the wild. Together with the Wildfowl Trust in Britain, the Hawaiian Board of Agriculture and Forestry started a captive breeding programme; initially the results were rather disappointing – but by 1955 things were looking up. By then there were probably more birds in captivity than in the wild, and over a third of the world's population was in England. In 1960, under carefully controlled conditions the first birds were released back into the wild, and in 1962 the first English-bred nénés were released. Thirty of them were released on the Island of Maui, where they had become extinct during the 19th century. Although it is still too early to claim the experiment as an unqualified success, there are now around 1,000 nénés in the world, distributed in many zoos as well as in the wild so it is safe to claim that this bird has at least been saved from extinction.

Fairy tern with chick. These delicate terns lay their single egg on the bare branch of a tree, and although many tumble down and perish, enough survive to maintain the population

Selected Reading List

Alexander, W. B. *Birds of the Ocean*, G. P. Putnam, New York, 1928.

Ali, Salim and Ripley, S. Dillon *Handbook of the Birds of India and Pakistan*, Oxford University Press, London, 1968 (10 volumes, uncompleted).

Bannerman, D. A. *Birds of West and Equatorial Africa*, Oliver & Boyd, Edinburgh, 1951–53 (two volumes).

Bond, James *Birds of the West Indies*, Collins, London, 1961.

Cave, F. O. and MacDonald, J. D. *Birds of the Sudan*, Oliver & Boyd, Edinburgh, 1955.

Cayley, N. W. *What Bird is That?*, Angus & Robertson, London, 1931, 4th edn. 1966; Tri-Ocean, San Francisco, 1966.

De Schauensee, R. M. *Guide to the Birds of South America*, Livingston Publishing, Wynnewood, Pa, USA, 1971.

Fisher, J., Simon, N., and Vincent, J. *The Red Book*, Collins, London, 1969.

Forshaw, J. *Australian Parrots*, Lansdowne Press, London, 1970.

Gilliard, E.T. *Birds of Paradise and Bower Birds*, Weidenfeld & Nicolson, London, 1969.

Gilliard, E.T. and Rand, A.L. *Handbook of New Guinea Birds*, Weidenfeld & Nicolson, London, 1967.

Gooders, J. (Ed.) *Birds of the World* (partwork), IPC Magazines, London, 1969–1971.

Goodwin, D. *Pigeons and Doves of the World*, British Museum (Natural History), London, 1967.

Greenaway, J.C. Jnr. *Extinct and Vanishing Birds of the World*, Dover Publications, New York, 1958. Distributed in Britain by Constable, London.

Haverschmidt, F. *Birds of Surinam*, Oliver & Boyd, Edinburgh, 1968; Livingston Publishing, Wynnewood, Pa, USA, 1968.

Henry, G.M. *Guide to the Birds of Ceylon*, Oxford University Press, London, 1955.

Immelmann, K. *Australian Finches*, Angus & Robertson, London, 1965; Tri-Ocean, San Francisco, 1965.

Landsborough-Thomson, A. (Ed.) *New Dictionary of Birds*, Thomas Nelson, London, 1964; McGraw-Hill, New York, 1964.

MacWorth-Praed, C.W. and Grant, C.H.B. *Handbook of African Birds*, Longman, London, 1952 onwards (6 volumes).

Prozesky, O.P.M. *Field Guide to the Birds of Southern Africa*, Collins, London, 1970.

Scheithauer, E. *Hummingbirds*, Arthur Barker, 1967; Thomas Crowell, New York, 1967.

Slater, P.S. *Field-guide to Australian Birds*, Oliver & Boyd, Edinburgh, 1971 (2 volumes).

Smythies, B.E. *Birds of Borneo*, Oliver & Boyd, Edinburgh, 1960.
Birds of Burma, Oliver & Boyd, Edinburgh, 1953.

Acknowledgments

Acknowledgments to photographs on the following pages: 2: Brian Coates/Bruce Coleman. 4,5,6,17: Len Robinson/Frank Lane. 7,22–23: Hans & Judy Beste/Ardea. 8 (top), 20 (top), 30–31: S.C. Bisserot/Bruce Coleman. 8 (bottom), 9: Root-Okapia. 10: Arthur Christiansen/Frank Lane. 11,38–39,52,54 (top),59,84,86 (right): Jane Burton/Bruce Coleman. 12,42,67, 103,107: Ardea. 13,21,26,27,91 (right): Bruce Coleman. 14: John Brownlie/Bruce Coleman. 15,19,20 (bottom): Graham Pizzey/Bruce Coleman. 16: W.R. Taylor/Ardea. 18: Eric Lindgren/ Ardea. 24: Wim Swaam/Camera Press. 28–29: C.P. Rose/Frank Lane. 29,33,34–35 (bottom), 71,89: Frank Lane. 32,34–35 (top), 36–37: S.C. Porter/Bruce Coleman. 40,45,87,92,106,114–115, 117, 119: Eric Hosking. 41: Frants Hartmann/Frank Lane. 43 (top): E. Hannmantha Rao/Natural History Photographic Agency. 43 (bottom), 58: Peter Jackson/Bruce Coleman. 44: John A. Burton. 47,77,102,108: Des & Jen Bartlett/Bruce Coleman. 48: G.D. Plage/Bruce Coleman. 49: P. Blasdale/ Ardea. 50 (top), 122,124,125: Peter Johnson/Natural History Photographic Agency. 50 (bottom): Lee Lyon/Bruce Coleman. 50–51 (top), 56–57: Leslie Brown/Ardea. 50–51 (bottom): Simon Trevor/Bruce Coleman. 52–53: C.K. Shah/Frank Lane. 54 (bottom), 66,78–79,79,80,82–83: Daniel Freeman. 55: Peter Steyn/Ardea. 60–61: R.S. Virdee/Frank Lane. 62: K.B. Newman/ Natural History Photographic Agency. 63,64: A.J. Deane/Bruce Coleman. 65: G.J. Brockhuysen/Ardea. 68,70: W.T. Miller/ Frank Lane. 69,72–73,76: R.M. Bloomfield/Ardea. 74: M.D. England/Ardea. 75: Cyril Laubscher/Bruce Coleman. 81: Patrick Boston/Natural Science Photos. 86 (left): Oxford Scientific Films/Bruce Coleman. 88: K.W. Fink/Ardea. 90,91 (left): C.A. Walker. 93,96: P. Morris/Ardea. 94–95 (top): Norman Myers/ Bruce Coleman. 94–95 (bottom): Gordon Langsbury/Bruce Coleman. 97: G.D. Plage/Bruce Coleman. 98–99: David Hughes/Bruce Coleman. 100: Francisco Erize/Bruce Coleman. 101: Su Gooders/Ardea. 104: T.W. Roth/Bruce Coleman. 105: T. Brosset/Natural Science Photos. 109: H. Schrempp/ Frank Lane. 110: George Laycock/Bruce Coleman. 112: A.M. Hutson. 113 (top): M.F. Soper/Bruce Coleman. 113 (bottom): John Pearson/Bruce Coleman. 116–117: M.P. Harris/Bruce Coleman. 118: R.W. Burton/Bruce Coleman. 120–121: Ron Taylor/Ardea. 123 (top), 123 (bottom): J.A. Hancock/Bruce Coleman. 126–127: Klaus Fiedler/Bruce Coleman.